TAKING CARE OF KITTENS

THE ULTIMATE "CAT PARENT'S" GUIDE TO RAISING A HAPPY AND HEALTHY FELINE

JULIAN NIVELLES

Modern Manifold
Publishing

To my dearest Mouse.
Without you, this book would not be possible

CONTENTS

INTRODUCTION

The smallest feline is a masterpiece

— LEONARDO DA VINCI

It was my wife Megan's birthday, and I wanted to do something special. She grew up with cats and always talked about how she loved raising them. So I thought to myself, what could be more special than adopting a furry little friend of our own? So, we decided to adopt a kitten. We found a listing on Craigslist in Phoenix, and after a quick chat on the phone, we headed off to pick her up. But when we saw her, we were a little taken aback. The poor little lynx point Siamese was covered in grease, her fur was all matted, and she was seriously underfed.

The whole exchange seemed to happen so fast that we didn't even have time to think, and before we knew it, we were driving home with a dirty kitten in a box. At first, she was shy and didn't seem to trust us, and to be honest, we weren't sure if we had made the right decision. But we knew we had to take care of her, so we gave her a good scrub and fed her some good grub. And let me tell you, the transformation was something else! She went from scruffy and unkempt to a beautiful white kitten with stunning blue eyes. We named her Mouse.

Over the next few days, Mouse slowly but surely settled into our family. She played with toys, snuggled with us, and explored every inch of our home. Before we knew it, she had captured our hearts and had become an integral part of our lives.

Adopting Mouse was one of the best decisions we've ever made. How much joy a little ball of fur can bring into your life is amazing. Sure, she was dirty and malnourished when we first saw her, but now she's a beloved member of our family.

OF CATS AND CULTURE

Our story is only one of many who have participated in the longstanding tradition of adopting cats into the household and integrating them into the family. In the United States, cats are the second most popular pet, following closely behind dogs, with approximately 46.5 million households owning at least one cat.[1]

Cats have shared a fascinating history with humans, serving as constant companions for thousands of years. As a result, they have played a significant role in cultural traditions and legends across the world, holding a special place in human society. From ancient Egypt to modern-day America, cats have been revered and adored for their unique personalities and mysterious behavior.

Throughout history, cats have been kept as pets for various reasons. In ancient Egypt, cats were worshipped as gods and were considered sacred animals. They were even mummified and buried with their owners to accompany them into the afterlife.[2]

Similarly, in Japan, Cats were considered so valuable that by the 10th century CE, only the nobility could afford to own one, and they were often housed in private pagodas.[3] In Norse mythology, felines held a significant place and were intricately linked with the revered goddess Freyja. The goddess was frequently portrayed with her two feline companions, who were said to accompany her and draw her chariot as she traversed through various realms.[4]

But beyond their cultural significance, cats have also played essential roles in shaping human history. In Scotland, cats were kept in distilleries to help control rodent populations and protect the precious grains used to make whiskey.[5] The most famous is Towser the Mouser, who lived at the Glenturret Distillery in Perthshire, Scotland. She was born in 1963 and spent her entire life at the distillery, patrolling the grounds and keeping them free of rodents. Towser gained worldwide fame for her remarkable mousing abilities, earning her a place in the

Guinness Book of World Records as the world's most prolific feline hunter.[6] It is estimated that she caught over 28,000 mice during her 24-year career at the distillery. Unfortunately, Towser passed away in 1987, but her memory lives on at the Glenturret Distillery, where she is honored with a statue and a special commemorative whisky.

The bond between cats and humans has been so strong that many writers, artists, and musicians have found inspiration in it. For example, Ernest Hemingway famously kept a colony of cats in his home in Key West, Florida. At the same time, T.S. Eliot wrote an entire book of poems, "*Old Possum's Book of Practical Cats,*" that later became the basis for the popular musical, "Cats." Even ancient poets such as Hafiz and William Blake have written about their love for their feline friends.

THE NECESSARY COMMITMENT

Bringing a kitten into your home is not just a decision to add a new pet to your family; it's also a continuation of this rich and fascinating relationship. By welcoming a kitten into your home, you become part of a community that spans cultures, countries, and centuries.

But taking care of a kitten is not just a walk in the park; some challenges and responsibilities come with raising one. Unfortunately, because of this, many cat owners choose to give up on their duties altogether.

According to the American Society for the Prevention of Cruelty to Animals (ASPCA), approximately 3.2 million cats enter U.S. animal shelters annually, and around 2.1 million are adopted. Unfortunately, about 530,000 cats are euthanized annually, meaning roughly 16.5% of cats entering shelters are euthanized.[7] These cats often experience poor welfare as they wait in shelters. But it doesn't have to be that way. With just a little education and commitment, you can gain the knowledge and confidence to care for your cat and contribute to a better world for all cats.

That's why I wrote this book - to guide you through every step, from preparing your home for your new kitten to raising and training them to keeping them healthy and happy for years to come.

WHAT TO EXPECT

Throughout this book, I'll cover various topics, from understanding kitten behavior and body language, choosing the right food and litter, and training and disciplining your kitten. We'll also discuss how to keep your kitten healthy, physically active, and mentally stimulated and provide tips for planning fun adventures with your new friend. We will also discuss a topic I am personally passionate about: The inhumane practice of declawing kittens and why prospect kitten owners should consider the risks before adopting.

But before diving into the practical tips and advice for raising a kitten, let's take a moment to appreciate the joy and laughter these little creatures can bring into our lives.

As Charles Dickens once said, "What greater gift than the love of a cat?" And it's true - there's something about the softness of their fur, the playfulness in their eyes, and the sweetness in their meows that can turn even the most challenging days into a moment of pure joy.

So, if you're ready to take the leap into kitten ownership or looking to improve your skills as a cat parent, Sit back, and let's embark on this journey together!

1. Statista. (n.d.). Pet ownership in the U.S. - statistics & facts. Retrieved from https://www.statista.com/topics/1258/pets/
2. Yuko, E. (2023, August 9). *How cats became divine symbols in ancient Egypt.* HISTORY. https://www.history.com/news/cats-ancient-egypt
3. Mark, J. J. (2022). Cats in the Ancient World. *World History Encyclopedia.* https://www.worldhistory.org/article/466/cats-in-the-ancient-world/
4. viking.style. (2023, December 1). *Freya and Her Feline Companions: The Cats of Norse Mythology - Viking Style.* Viking Style. https://viking.style/freya-and-her-feline-companions-the-cats-of-norse-mythology/
5. Bell, E. (2021, May 7). *The secret history of distillery cats.* VinePair. https://vinepair.com/articles/history-jameson-distillery-cats/
6. *Greatest mouser.* (n.d.). Guinness World Records. https://www.guinnessworldrecords.com/world-records/greatest-mouser
7. American Society for the Prevention of Cruelty to Animals. (n.d.). Pet statistics. https://www.aspca.org/helping-people-pets/shelter-intake-and-surrender/pet-statistics

KITTENS 101: THE BASICS

> There are two means of refuge from the miseries of life: music and cats
>
> — ALBERT SCHWEITZER

L et me tell you a story about my buddy Jerry, who decided to adopt a kitten on a whim. He thought it would be a piece of cake, but boy, was he wrong!

On his first day with his new kitten, Jerry realized he was unprepared. He had no food, no litter box, and no toys or scratching post. In a moment of desperation, he gave the little furball some leftover Chinese takeout, only to quickly regret it. The kitten promptly vomited all over Jerry's brand-new sofa, leaving him in a state of shock.

But that was just the beginning of Jerry's problems. The kitten, driven by its natural instincts, proceeded to use a pile of Jerry's clothes as a makeshift litter box, leaving a mess everywhere. And as if that wasn't enough, the little troublemaker then started to scratch every piece of furniture in sight, starting and ending with the already-vomit-covered sofa.

Jerry tried to discipline the kitten, but it seemed to thrive on the challenge, scratching faster and harder while staring at Jerry defiantly. It was as if the kitten was saying, "Bring it on!" to Jerry's feeble attempts to stop it.

In conclusion, Jerry's first day with his new kitten was a disaster, but it was also a valuable lesson. He quickly learned that taking care of a kitten requires preparation, patience, and a whole lot of cleaning up.

He learned he needed to stock up on kitten food, litter, toys, and scratch posts. He also realized he needed to kitten-proof his apartment by covering electrical cords and hiding breakable items. Plus, he had to schedule a visit to the vet because kittens need vaccinations, check-ups, and the dreaded spaying or neutering.

So, future kitten owners, please don't be like my friend Jerry. Instead, do your research, gather all the necessary supplies, and kitten-proof your home before bringing home your new furry friend. Trust me, it will save you a lot of headaches and vomit-covered sofas.

ESSENTIAL GEAR

Now, if you've decided to adopt a kitten, congratulations! It's an exciting time, but preparing appropriately is essential to ensure a smooth transition for you and your new furry friend. This chapter will explain creating a kitten-friendly home ready for your kitten's arrival.

Before we move on in the chapter, I will discuss various gear you may want to purchase for your new kitten. For your convenience, I've compiled a list of recommended kitten gear that may be helpful for you to reference and follow along with. To assist you, I have thoughtfully arranged the various options based on their price range. So whether you want to be budget or bougie, this list will have something for you. From toys and scratching posts to litter boxes and carriers, this list has got you covered.

But that's not all! To make things even easier for you, you can download the free PDF by scanning the below QR code!

Download the guide today and start shopping for your new kitten's essentials before they arrive!

STARTING FROM THE BEGINNING

First things first, when looking for a kitten to adopt and planning to do it through a private exchange such as Craig's List or Facebook marketplace, it is crucial that you do not take home a kitten that is less than eight weeks old. Taking kittens away from their mothers and littermates too early can adversely affect their physical and emotional health. Kittens separated from their mother and siblings before they're eight weeks old may miss out on essential nutrients and antibodies from their mother's milk, making them more susceptible to illnesses and infections.[1]

Moreover, being with their mother and littermates helps kittens develop essential social and behavioral skills. They learn to communicate with other cats, establish boundaries, and play appropriately. These skills are critical for a cat's long-term well-being, as they'll need them to interact with other cats and humans throughout their lives.

We're giving them the best chance at a healthy and happy life by waiting until the kittens are at least eight weeks old before separating them from their mother and littermates, making them more well-adjusted and better equipped to handle life's challenges.

BRINGING YOUR KITTEN HOME

Now that we've got that out of the way let's talk about creating a kitten-friendly home. Before bringing your kitten home, assess your living space to ensure it's safe and comfortable. If you live in a small apartment or have limited space, provide enough room for your kitten to play and explore.

Kittens are curious creatures and love to explore their surroundings, so remove any toxic plants or substances that could harm your kitten. In addition, loose electrical cords and other potential hazards should be secured or removed to prevent accidents.

CHOOSING THE RIGHT SUPPLIES FOR YOUR KITTEN

Before bringing a new kitten home, it's essential to make sure you have all the necessary supplies to ensure they are comfortable and well-cared for.

The first item on your list should be a litter box. We will talk more about litter box training in Chapter 4; for now, just know that kittens are naturally clean animals and will quickly learn how to use a litter box, but you need to provide them with an appropriate size and type of litter box. Consider getting a low-sided litter box so it's easy for your kitten to climb in and out of, and fill it with good quality, unscented litter.

Food and water bowls are also essential items for your new kitten. I will talk later in this chapter about getting a motorized water fountain instead of a water bowl, but if you're not ready for the running fountain, a bowl will do for now. Opt for shallow, sturdy bowls that won't tip over easily. Kitten-specific bowls are often smaller and more accessible for your kitten to eat; some even come with built-in slow feeders to help prevent overeating.

Providing a scratching post is crucial for your kitten's well-being, allowing them to scratch and stretch, satisfying their natural instincts. Choose a scratching post tall enough for your kitten to stretch out fully, and make sure it's sturdy and stable. If you don't want to buy a scratching post because you plan to declaw your kitten, please **STOP READING** and skip to Chapter 8 of this book before moving forward.

Finally, a carrier is essential for transporting your kitten. Choose a carrier that is the appropriate size for your kitten and has plenty of ventilation and security features. If you plan on flying with your kitten, consider opting for a TSA-approved carrying case.

When choosing supplies for your new kitten, it is vital to ensure they are designed for kittens and are the appropriate size. This will ensure that your kitten is comfortable and safe and will help them adjust to their new home quickly and easily. In addition, by having all the necessary supplies on hand, you'll be able to focus on bonding with your new kitten and providing them with the love and care they need.

SELECTING NUTRITIOUS AND DELICIOUS KITTEN FOOD

When it comes to feeding your new kitten, the topic of food can quickly become a point of contention. You may be thinking, "Don't I just have to buy a bag of dry kitten kibble?" However, as we delve deeper into the world of feline nutrition in Chapter 3, we'll discover that the answer is more complex than you would initially think. With debates raging over whether dry kibble, wet food, or a raw diet is the best option, it's easy to feel overwhelmed.

It's essential to remember that cats have evolved from their wild ancestors to eat a very specific diet, which we'll explore in greater detail in Chapter 3. For now, just know that I will argue there is a spectrum of foods that are best to worst for your kitten's health, with a raw diet coming out on top and dry kibble ranking as the least desirable option. While the raw diet has its supporters, there are also concerns about the risks it poses to both cats and their human caretakers. So, for now, we'll focus on wet food as an optimal middle ground for the convenience of new kitten owners.

In general, kittens should eat wet food whenever possible. This is because wet food is more natural, contains higher protein and moisture levels, and can help prevent many common feline health problems. But, of course, not all wet food is created equal, and choosing a high-quality brand that provides a balanced and complete nutritional profile is essential. With that in mind, let's take a closer look at selecting the best wet food for your new feline friend.

GENERAL WET FOOD GUIDANCE

When it comes to feeding your kitten, it's important to remember that they have different nutritional needs than adult cats. Kittens require more protein, fat, and calories to support their growth and development.[2] Therefore, choosing a high-quality kitten food that provides all the necessary nutrients for their specific requirements is essential.

When selecting a kitten food, look for a brand specifically formulated for kittens. These foods are designed to provide the right balance of nutrients that kittens need for healthy growth and development. In addition, some kitten food brands include additional nutrients like DHA (Docosahexaenoic Acid), which is essential for brain and vision development.

It's also essential to choose a food that includes high-quality protein sources. Look for brands that use real meat, poultry, or fish as the first ingredient. Avoid brands that contain fillers like corn, wheat, or soy, as these ingredients do not provide the necessary nutrients and can be difficult for kittens to digest.

To ensure that you are feeding your kitten high-quality food that meets their specific nutritional needs, it's a good idea to talk to your veterinarian. They can recommend the best brands and formulas based on your kitten's needs and provide guidance on feeding amounts and schedules.

In addition to choosing the right food, it's essential to ensure your kitten has access to clean, fresh water at all times. Kittens love running water, so consider getting a motorized fountain to drink from. These fountains help to encourage cats to drink more water, which is vital for their overall health and well-being. I'll talk more about why in chapter 3, but for now, just trust me that you will want to invest in a motorized water fountain. Kittens are prone to dehydration, so they must drink enough water to support their overall health.

PREPARING FOR YOUR FIRST VISIT TO THE VET

We will talk later about choosing the right veterinarian, but for now, know that your kitten will need to visit the veterinarian shortly after you bring them home. This initial visit is crucial for your kitten's health, including a physical exam, vaccinations, and a check for parasites. However, it's common for kittens to be afraid of the vet due to unfamiliar surroundings and experiences. Therefore, it's essential to make the visit as stress-free as possible for your kitten so they don't develop a fear of the vet in the future.

To help ease your kitten's fear of the vet, you can help prepare them for the vet by handling them regularly and getting them used to being touched in different areas of their body, such as their paws, ears, and tail. This will help them feel more comfortable during the physical exam.

Additionally, you can make the trip to the vet less stressful by placing your kitten in a comfortable carrier and covering it with a familiar blanket. This can provide a sense of security for your kitten and help them feel more at ease. Finally, consider using taste aversives, such as bitter apple spray, on your hands or gloves to discourage your kitten from biting or scratching during the exam.

Lastly, it's important to note that pet insurance can help cover the cost of future veterinary care for your kitten. Before bringing your kitten home, consider researching different pet insurance options to find a plan that fits your budget and provides the coverage you need. By taking these steps, you can help ensure that your kitten receives the necessary veterinary care and remains healthy and happy for years to come.

TRANSPORTING YOUR KITTEN

Transporting your kitten can be a stressful experience, so it's important to prioritize their safety and comfort during the journey. If your kitten gets anxious during car rides, there are a few things you can do to help ease their stress. One option is to talk to your vet about anti-anxiety medication or natural remedies.[3] However, it is essential to consult your vet before administering any medication to your kitten. Another option is to play music during the ride. Studies show cats respond well to music with a slow tempo and low-pitched tones. This can help soothe your kitten and make the ride more enjoyable.

Pro Tip: Search for "music for cats" on

any music service and play it in
the car

When introducing a new kitten to your home, decreasing any initial anxiety between them and any existing pets is vital. Using a crate, leash, and harness can help control the cats during initial introductions.[4] Keeping the new kitten in its own area and allowing introductions when the cats eat, or play is also recommended. Additionally, a synthetic cheek gland scent can help ease the transition for the new kitten.

THE BENEFITS OF MICROCHIPPING

Microchipping your kitten can have numerous benefits. The most significant advantage of microchipping is that it increases the chances of reuniting with your lost pet. When paired with the correct contact information, a microchip can help locate your kitten if it gets lost.[5]

Microchipping is a safe and permanent way to identify your pet. Unlike a collar or a tag, a microchip cannot be easily removed, lost, or damaged, and it doesn't cause discomfort to your kitten. The microchip is implanted under the skin, typically between the shoulder blades, and can be read by a scanner that most animal shelters, veterinary clinics, and rescue organizations have.

Another advantage of microchipping your kitten is that it can help prevent pet theft. For example, thieves may steal kittens to sell or use them for breeding. However, if your kitten is microchipped, it can be easily identified as your pet, making it harder for thieves to sell or use them for nefarious purposes. Additionally, if someone finds your lost kitten and takes her to a veterinarian or an animal shelter, the microchip can quickly identify you as the owner.

Finally, microchipping your kitten can save you money and time. If your kitten is lost and picked up by animal control or taken to an animal shelter, they will scan it for a microchip. If your kitten has a microchip, you will be contacted immediately and reunited with your kitten. This will save you the expense of paying fees and fines that come with reclaiming your pet from an animal shelter.

NICE TO HAVES

If you want to spoil your furry feline friend with a few extra goodies, here are some purr-fectly delightful items that will make your kitten's life even more enjoyable! While optional, these are worth considering if you want to go the extra mile to provide the ultimate kitty experience.

- **Cat Tree:** A cat tree would be a great addition to a home with kittens for several reasons. Firstly, kittens are naturally curious and love to climb and explore their surroundings. A cat tree provides a safe and comfortable place to climb, perch, and play, satisfying their natural instincts while keeping them entertained and engaged. Secondly, a cat tree can help kittens to develop their balance, coordination, and agility. As they climb up and down the tree, they build their muscles and improve their motor skills. This is especially important for indoor kittens, who may not have as many opportunities to exercise and play as outdoor cats.

Thirdly, a cat tree can provide a space for kittens to rest and relax. Kittens need plenty of rest to support their growth and development, and a cat tree offers a cozy and comfortable spot for them to nap.

- **Toys:** Toys are not just for playtime but also for a kitten's mental and physical development. Interactive toys like feather wands, balls, and puzzles can provide your kitten with mental stimulation and promote exercise, keeping them healthy and happy. Having a variety of toys available can also help prevent destructive behavior, as your kitten will have an outlet for their energy and curiosity. Toys are also great for bonding with your kitten and can provide hours of entertainment for you and your furry friend.

- **Grooming Brush:** Brushing your kitten regularly can help keep their coat healthy and shiny, prevent hairballs, and provide a bonding experience for you and your kitten. Brushing also helps distribute natural oils throughout their coat, keeping their skin moisturized and preventing dryness. You may need a specific brush, depending on your kitten's coat type. For example, long-haired kittens may require a slicker brush or comb, while short-haired kittens may do well with a soft-bristled brush. Regular grooming with a brush can make a big difference in your kitten's overall health and appearance.

- **Bedding:** A soft and plush bed provides a warm and secure spot for your kitten to rest and sleep, which is important for their development and overall health. Look for a machine-washable bed that is easy to clean, as kittens may have accidents or spills… I know this from experience… A good bed can also help reduce anxiety and stress, providing your kitten with a sense of security and comfort.

- **Collar and ID tag:** A collar and ID tag are essential for your kitten's safety, especially if they are outdoor or indoor-outdoor cats. An ID tag with your kitten's name and your contact information can help them find their way home if they get lost. Also, use a breakaway collar that will release if your kitten gets caught on something, preventing injury or strangulation. A collar and ID tag are also great for identifying your kitten as a pet, especially if they have health conditions or special needs.
- **Body harness and leash:** A body harness and leash can provide a safe and controlled way for your kitten to explore the outdoors. A harness is better than a collar, as it distributes pressure more evenly and prevents choking or injury. Before taking your kitten outside, ensure they are up to date on their vaccinations and that the area is safe and free from hazards.

CONCLUSION

Adopting a kitten is a big deal and takes some serious prep and responsibility. You gotta understand what these little fur-balls need to live their best lives. Kitten-proof your home, get the necessary supplies, feed them the right food, and take them to the vet. Trust me, doing your homework will make a smoother transition for you and your new kitty pal. And listen, adopting a kitten means a long-term commitment, but the love and joy they bring into your life are priceless.

In the next chapter, we will get to know our kittens better, and I'm talking beyond just their cute little faces. We'll delve into their behavior and body language to better communicate with our furry friends. We'll also talk about bonding with your kitten through play, creating routines, and discovering what they like and dislike. So, let's get ready to have some fun and learn how to speak the language of the meows.

1. Leeson, J. (2023, July 21). *When can kittens leave their mom? How to tell if they're ready.* The Dog People by Rover.com. https://www.rover.com/blog/when-can-kittens-leave-mom/
2. Stuart, A. (2009, July 16). *Feeding kittens: What, when, how much.* WebMD. https://www.webmd.com/pets/cats/features/feeding-your-kitten-food-and-treats
3. Grota, J., DVM. (2023, December 14). *8 Tips For Traveling with a Cat.* PetMD. https://www.petmd.com/cat/care/8-tips-traveling-cat
4. Berger, J. (2023, October 23). *How to introduce a new kitten to your home.* PetMD. https://www.petmd.com/cat/care/best-ways-introduce-new-kitten-your-home
5. Mick, L. (2023, September 19). *Why you should microchip your cat.* PetMD. https://www.petmd.com/cat/general-health/why-microchip-cats

2

PAWSOME COMMUNICATION: UNDERSTANDING YOUR KITTEN'S LANGUAGE AND NEEDS

Owners of dogs will have noticed that, if you provide them with food and water and shelter and affection, they will think you are God. Whereas owners of cats are compelled to realize that, if you provide them with food and water and affection, they draw the conclusion that they are God

— CHRISTOPHER HITCHENS

> A cat has absolute emotional honesty. Human beings, for one reason or another, may hide their feelings, but a cat does not

— ERNEST HEMINGWAY

Let's face it - cats and dogs might both be four-legged, furry creatures, but that's where the similarities end. For starters, cats are much more independent creatures than dogs. While dogs are known for their loyalty and desire to please their owners, cats tend to be more self-sufficient and prefer to do things on their terms. As a result, they're less likely to follow commands or engage in training exercises, and they're not as inclined to seek out human attention.

One of the most significant differences between cats and dogs is their communication styles. Dogs are known for being vocal animals who bark, growl, and whine to express their emotions. On the other hand, cats are typically more subtle in their communication. They might meow, purr, or hiss but also use body language, such as tail flicks or ear positions, to convey their feelings. It can be challenging for people to understand their kitten's behavior since they often use nuanced and subtle forms of communication.

If you treat your kitten like a dog, you might be expecting them to act in ways that are not natural to them. For example, while some kittens might enjoy playing fetch, most aren't as interested in this activity as dogs are. Similarly, some kittens might not appreciate being hugged or held tightly, which many dogs enjoy. If you force your kitten to do things against their nature, you will likely frustrate yourself and your kitten.

So, if you want to have a happy and fulfilling relationship with your furry feline friend, it's essential to take the time to understand their unique language and behavior. We'll start by laying a solid foundation of knowledge and learning how your kitten's breed plays a role in their communication style. From there, we'll dive into the fascinating world of feline vocalizations and decode the different meows, hisses, and purrs your kitten uses to express themselves. And let's not forget the importance of non-verbal communication! We'll explore how to read your kitten's body language, including even the most subtle of physical cues. By becoming fluent in the language of cats, you'll be able to communicate with your kitten on a deeper level, strengthen your bond, and enjoy a happier and more fulfilling relationship. So, let's embark on this journey together and become experts in feline communication!

TEMPERAMENTS: UNDERSTANDING YOUR KITTEN'S UNIQUE PERSONALITY

Before delving into kitten behavior and communication, it's crucial to have a solid foundation of understanding about your kitten's breed. It's true - just like people, different breeds of cats can have distinct personality traits and tendencies. If you're considering adopting a kitten, it's important to consider the typical temperament of its breed.

SIAMESE

Siamese cats are one of the most popular cat breeds in the world. They are known for their striking blue eyes and elegant appearance. Siamese cats are vocal and social and are often described as loving and loyal companions. They crave attention from their owners and love to be around people. They have a reputation for being talkative and often converse with their owners. Siamese cats are also very intelligent and can learn to do tricks and even walk on a leash.

However, they are active and need plenty of playtime and exercise to stay happy and healthy. If they don't get enough attention, they may resort to destructive behavior, such as scratching furniture or chewing on cords.

PERSIAN

Persian cats are one of the oldest cat breeds and have been around for centuries. They are known for their long, fluffy coats and calm demeanor. Persian cats are gentle and affectionate, and they make excellent lap cats. They are often described as "couch potatoes" because they enjoy lounging around and taking it easy. Persian cats are devoted to their owners and form strong bonds with them. However, Persian cats can be a bit shy around strangers. They may take time to warm up to new people and environments. They also require a lot of grooming to keep their long coats looking beautiful. Owners must be prepared to devote a lot of time to grooming their Persian cats to prevent the matting and tangling of their fur.

MAINE COON

Maine Coon cats are one of the largest domesticated cat breeds. They are often called "gentle giants" because of their size and friendly demeanor. Maine Coon cats are playful and sociable, and they get along well with children and other pets. They are known for their loyalty and devotion to their owners. Maine Coon cats are also very intelligent and can learn to do tricks and even walk on a leash. They are active and love to play, so owners must provide plenty of toys and playtime to keep them happy and healthy. Maine Coon cats also have thick, luxurious coats that require regular grooming to prevent matting.

SPHYNX

Sphynx cats are a unique breed with a hairless appearance. Despite their lack of fur, Sphynx cats are energetic and playful. They crave attention from their owners and enjoy cuddling. Sphynx cats are also very social and get along well with children and other pets. However, Sphynx cats have no fur, meaning they can be sensitive to temperature changes. Therefore, owners must be careful to keep them warm in cooler weather. Sphynx cats also require regular bathing to keep their skin clean and healthy. For these reasons, Sphynx cats are generally considered to be a "high-maintenance" breed.

BENGAL

Bengal cats are a high-energy breed that requires lots of mental and physical stimulation to keep them happy and healthy. They are intelligent and curious, and they love to explore their surroundings. Bengal cats are also very athletic and can be trained to do tricks and even walk on a leash. However, Bengal cats can be very vocal and may become destructive if they don't receive enough stimulation. Therefore, owners must provide plenty of toys and playtime to keep them entertained. Unfortunately, Bengal cats are also known for their strong prey drive, so they may not be a good fit for households with small animals.

SCOTTISH FOLD

Scottish Fold cats are known for their distinctive folded ears and sweet personalities. They are loyal to their owners and enjoy playing and cuddling. Scottish Fold cats are adaptable and thrive in various environments, from apartments to larger homes. However, Scottish Fold cats can be prone to health issues related to their folded ears. Therefore, owners must be prepared to provide extra care and attention to their ears to prevent infections and other problems. Scottish Fold cats also require regular grooming to keep their coat healthy and free from matting.

CHAUSIE

Chausie cats are a relatively new breed originating from a cross between domestic and jungle cats. They are often described as intelligent and outgoing and enjoy exploring their environment. Chausie cats are also very active and require plenty of exercises to keep them happy and healthy. They may even enjoy playing fetch with their owners. However, because of their wild ancestry, Chausie cats can be more challenging to train than other domesticated cat breeds. They also require a lot of mental stimulation to prevent boredom and destructive behavior.

Understanding your kitten's breed-specific temperament can help read their body language and behavior. But, of course, it's important to remember that each kitten is an individual with its own unique personality, regardless of breed. By spending time with your kitten and observing its behavior, you can better understand its likes, dislikes, and quirks in order to build a strong bond of love and companionship.

THE CAT'S MEOW: DECIPHERING THE VOCAL LANGUAGE OF KITTENS"

Cat vocalizations are one of the most fascinating aspects of feline behavior. From the gentle purr to the fierce hiss, cats have a variety of ways to communicate with their owners and other felines. This section will explore three of the most common cat vocalizations: the meow, the purr, and the hiss. We will delve into the different meanings behind each sound and discuss the situations in which cats are most likely to use them. Whether you're a seasoned cat owner or adopting your first kitten, this section will provide valuable insights into feline communication.

THE MEOW

Kittens can be pretty vocal creatures, especially when it comes to their signature meows. Meowing is a type of communication kittens and adult cats use to communicate with humans. Cats meow for various reasons, including seeking attention, expressing hunger, or communicating discomfort or pain. In addition, cats may also meow as a greeting, to express playfulness or excitement, or to indicate fear or aggression.

But did you know that meowing is actually not a natural form of communication for cats? In the wild, cats communicate with each other using body language, scents, and other vocalizations like hisses and growls. However, through domestication and evolution, cats have learned to meow specifically to communicate with humans. Interestingly, kittens are the only ones who meow at each other, and they typically do so to communicate with their mother. However, as cats mature and become more independent, they begin to meow less frequently with each other and more often with their human companions.[1]

While meowing is a common behavior among cats, paying attention to any changes in your cat's vocalizations is essential, as it may be a sign of an underlying health issue or behavioral problem. If you notice any unusual changes in your cat's meowing, it's always a good idea to consult your veterinarian to ensure your feline friend is healthy and happy.

THE PURR

One of the most recognizable kitten vocalizations is the purr. It's a sound that can warm even the coldest of hearts and instantly puts one at ease. But have you ever wondered why kittens purr?

The origins of the feline purr have long been a subject of scientific interest and debate. While the exact mechanism behind purring is still not entirely understood, a 1991 study by Elizabeth von Muggenthaler found that purring is a product of the cat's voice box or larynx.[2]

According to this study, when a cat breathes, it dilates and constricts the glottis, the area around its vocal cords, in a rapid, rhythmic fashion. The purring sound occurs as the air vibrates over the laryngeal muscles of the cat's larynx. This suggests that the purring mechanism is a voluntary act controlled by the cat's respiratory system.

Further research has shown that cats have a unique purring frequency range, between 25 and 150 Hertz, which can promote healing and relaxation in both cats and humans. In addition, these frequencies are thought to stimulate the healing of bones, muscles, and other tissues, reducing pain and inflammation.

Interestingly, purring may also serve as a means of communication between cats and humans. While cats may purr when they are happy or relaxed, they may also purr when in pain or anxious, indicating that they may be seeking comfort or assistance from their human companions.

Even though purring has been observed in domestic cats and some wild cats, not all felines possess this ability. For instance, lions, tigers, and jaguars cannot purr due to differences in their vocal anatomy. The only exception to this rule is the snow leopard, which has been found to have a unique vocalization that is sometimes referred to as a "purr."

The enigmatic purr highlights the complexity of the feline-human relationship, which continues to intrigue scientists and cat lovers alike. In addition, it's a reminder that these creatures are not just cute and cuddly but possess a unique physiology and communication system that sets them apart from all other animals.

THE HISS

Hissing is a sound that can send chills down your spine. It's a sharp, sudden noise that can signal fear, anger, or desire to be left alone. But did you know that hissing is actually an involuntary reaction for cats? It's not something they choose to do but rather a natural response when they feel threatened or uncomfortable.[3]

Hissing is a defense mechanism for cats that can ward off potential attackers, whether other cats, dogs, or humans. It's a warning sign that says, "Back off, or you'll regret it!" And while it might be scary for humans to hear, it's an integral part of a cat's communication repertoire.

In addition to being a warning sign, hissing can be a way

for cats to express their discomfort or pain. For example, if a cat is experiencing sudden discomforts, such as from a medical issue or injury, it may hiss as a way to communicate its distress.

While hissing may not be the most pleasant sound to hear, it's essential to understand that it's a natural and necessary part of a cat's communication. By paying attention to your cat's body language and signals, such as flattened ears or an arched back, you can help avoid situations that might lead to hissing and create a safe and comfortable environment.

SCRATCHING THE SURFACE: UNDERSTANDING YOUR KITTEN'S BODY LANGUAGE AND BEHAVIORS

THE TAIL

Beginning with arguably the most visual communication asset a kitten has... the tale. These versatile tools help kittens express a range of emotions, from happiness to fear to aggression.[4] Understanding the messages a kitten's tail sends can help us better understand them and communicate more effectively.

One of the most common tail positions kittens use to communicate is the upright tail. This position indicates that the kitten feels confident, happy, and alert. When a kitten is in this position, its tail is usually straight up in the air and may be slightly curved at the tip. This position indicates that the kitten is feeling good and open to social interaction.

On the other hand, a kitten that is fearful or threatened will often tuck its tail between its legs or wrap it around its body. This position indicates that the kitten is anxious or defensive and may be preparing to flee or attack. Therefore, a kitten with a tucked tail should be cautiously approached and given plenty of space.

A kitten's tail can also indicate its level of arousal or excitement. For example, when a kitten feels playful or engaged, its tail may twitch or swish rapidly. This behavior indicates that the kitten is ready to play and may be trying to get your attention.

Finally, a kitten's tail can also indicate its level of aggression or irritation. For example, when a kitten feels threatened or annoyed, its tail may lash back and forth or hold it low to the ground. This behavior indicates that the kitten feels defensive and may prepare to attack.

Overall, a kitten's tail is a handy tool for communication. By observing your kitten's tail position and movements, you can better understand its emotional state and communicate with it more effectively. Whether your kitten feels happy, anxious, playful, or defensive, its tail will provide essential clues to help you make the connection.

THE EARS

A cat's ears are one of their most impressive features. Their ears are highly mobile and are an essential survival tool for hunting prey and detecting danger.

Beyond their physical function, cats' ears also reveal their moods and intentions. When a cat is alert and interested, their ears will be pointed forward and slightly tilted, indicating its curiosity and attention. Conversely, when a cat feels scared or threatened, their ears will flatten against its head, communicating its defensive or aggressive posture. Even when a cat is relaxed and content, their ears may be slightly turned to the side or held up but not rigidly, reflecting its peaceful state.

Cats can also use their ears to communicate with other cats. For example, when feeling aggressive or threatened, a cat may flatten their ears as a warning to stay away. In contrast, when they are playing or grooming, their ears may be relaxed but alert, showing their trust and friendliness.

The mobility and expressiveness of cats' ears make them essential for communication and survival. Understanding their movements and positions can provide valuable insights into their emotions and behaviors.

THE "HALLOWEEN CAT" POSE

When a kitten or cat walks with its back arched and tail puffed up, it is often called the Halloween cat pose. This pose is a clear sign that the kitten is scared or threatened and trying to make itself appear larger and more intimidating to potential predators.

The Halloween cat pose is also often accompanied by sideways walking, where the kitten or cat moves with a sideways motion rather than a straight-ahead gait. This movement is also a defensive behavior, as it allows the kitten to keep its eyes on potential threats while moving in a defensive posture.

If you notice your kitten or cat walking in the Halloween cat pose, it's crucial to approach it with caution and give it plenty of space. This pose indicates that the kitten feels scared or threatened and may lash out or become aggressive if it feels cornered.

To help your kitten feel more comfortable and secure, try

creating a safe and inviting environment to retreat to. For example, provide plenty of hiding spots and cozy beds, and avoid loud noises or sudden movements that could startle the kitten. Over time, your kitten will likely grow more comfortable and confident in its environment and may even lose the Halloween cat pose altogether.

MAKING BISCUITS "KNEADING"

Watching a kitten knead with its paws (or, as we say in our household, "making biscuits") can be an incredibly endearing sight, and it turns out that this behavior is not only cute but also serves a meaningful purpose. Kneading is a natural behavior that kittens learn when nursing from their mother, and it can be a sign of affection, comfort, and contentment.

When kittens nurse from their mother, they instinctively knead their paws against her mammary glands. This behavior stimulates the milk flow and helps the kitten get the nourishment needed to grow and thrive. Over time, kittens come to associate this behavior with feelings of comfort and security and will often continue to knead well into adulthood.

Kneading can be a sign of affection from a kitten to its human, and many cats will knead their owners to show their love and trust. In addition, when a kitten kneads with its paws, it's often accompanied by purring, another sign of contentment and relaxation.

Interestingly, kneading can also serve as a way for kittens to mark their territory. This is because cats have scent glands in their paws, and kneading can release their scent onto the surface they're kneading on, marking it as their own.

If your kitten is kneading, it's important to be gentle and patient. Kneading can be a vulnerable behavior, and your kitten may stop if it feels uncomfortable or threatened. You can encourage your kitten to knead by providing a soft, comfortable surface for it to knead on, such as a blanket or a plush pillow.

SCRATCHING

Now, when it comes to common kitten behaviors like biting and scratching during playtime, it's essential to train them to distinguish between play and aggression to avoid injuries.

When cats scratch furniture, it's not always because they are trying to be destructive. In fact, it's a natural behavior that serves several important purposes for them. For example, scratching helps keep their claws healthy and sharp, removes the dead outer layer of their nails, and helps stretch and tone their muscles.

But scratching also has a social component for cats. When they scratch, they leave behind their scent and visual marks that communicate to other cats that this territory is claimed. In some cases, when a cat is particularly attached to their owner, they may also scratch furniture to mix their scent with their owner's, creating a sense of shared ownership and belonging. So, while it can be frustrating to see your furniture being damaged, it's essential to understand that scratching is a natural and necessary behavior for cats, and providing them with appropriate scratching surfaces can help redirect their behavior and preserve your furniture.

But beyond scratching furniture, cats can also use their

claws as defensive weapons. Cats are natural predators and have a strong instinct to protect themselves from potential threats. One way they do this is by scratching as a form of self-defense. When a cat feels threatened or cornered, it may lash out with its claws to protect itself.

By providing your kitten with safe and secure environments and plenty of mental and physical stimulation, we can help our feline companions feel more relaxed and less threatened, reducing the likelihood of scratching behavior.

BITING

Cats can be fascinating creatures with their playful and curious personalities. However, sometimes their behavior can turn aggressive, resulting in painful bites to humans and other cats. Understanding the reasons behind their biting behavior is essential to build a healthy relationship with them.

One type of biting behavior that cats may exhibit is "love bites." These playful nibbles often show affection towards their owners or feline companions but can also indicate over-stimulation.[5] Imagine your cat giving you a little love nibble when they're feeling particularly playful - it's their way of showing that they care!

On the other hand, cats may also bite when they feel threatened, in pain, or uncomfortable. This is especially important to remember when introducing a new cat into the household, as cats are territorial animals and may bite to defend their territory or establish dominance.

It's crucial to socialize your cat at a young age and reward good behavior to prevent cats from biting. In addition, attention to your cat's body language and signals, such as flattened ears or a twitching tail, can help you understand when they feel threatened or uncomfortable. And if you do get bitten, make sure to clean the wound thoroughly and seek medical attention if necessary.

SLOW BLINKING

Some people assume that when a cat slowly blinks, they are aloof or uninterested in their surroundings. However, this couldn't be further from the truth. Slow blinking is, in fact, a powerful signal of a cat's comfort and relaxation. By slowly closing and opening their eyes, cats convey that they feel safe and secure in their environment and are at ease in the presence of their humans. This is particularly noteworthy since, in the wild, cats must always be alert for potential threats.[6]

Slow-blinking is a powerful tool for building trust and strengthening the bond between humans and felines. This behavior is often accompanied by other signs of relaxation, such as a lowered tail and relaxed body posture. Moreover, slow blinking can also demonstrate affection. When a kitten slow-blinks at you, it shows they love and trust you. In return, if you slowly blink back at your kitten, it can help strengthen your bond and show them that you care for them too.

Slow blinking is a simple but powerful tool for building trust and understanding between you and your kitten. Responding to your kitten's slow blinks with slow blinks of your own can help establish a sense of communication and understanding that goes beyond words. This technique can be particularly beneficial for shy or anxious kittens, helping to build their confidence and make them feel more comfortable in their environment.

ZOOMIES

At some point, you will see your kitten suddenly burst into a wild sprint around the house, leaping over furniture and running up and down the stairs. This frenzied behavior, known as the "zoomies," is common among kittens and is entirely normal.

The reason for the "zoomies" is simply a burst of energy that needs to be released. Kittens have a lot of energy to burn; sometimes, they need to let it all out.

In addition to burning off energy, the "zoomies" can also serve as a stress reliever for kittens. Just like humans, kittens can experience stress and anxiety, and the sudden burst of activity can help to alleviate those feelings.

So, if you see your kitten running around like crazy, don't worry - it's just the "zoomies"! Just make sure to provide plenty of opportunities for play and exercise to help them release their energy healthily and safely. However, you may find that kittens tend to do this at night while you're sleeping. To prevent this, you must establish a routine with your kitten. We will talk more about that in Chapter 5.

CONCLUSION

While all kittens share some common communication behaviors, such as meowing, purring, and hissing, every cat is a unique individual with its own personality and preferences. Factors such as breed, upbringing, socialization, and life experiences can all influence a cat's communication style and behavior. Therefore, it's important to get to know your kitten and observe their individual communication patterns to better understand their needs and preferences. But don't fret; it's not rocket science!

Take the time to learn about your kitty's unique needs and personality traits. Then, from breed-specific quirks to distinguishing between playful and aggressive behavior, you can create a safe and happy home for your kitten to thrive in.

In the next chapter, we'll dive into the nitty-gritty of kitty care. We'll cover everything from common health issues to nutrition and exercise. So buckle up, folks, and get ready to be the best cat parent ever!

1. American Society for the Prevention of Cruelty to Animals. (n.d.). *Meowing and yowling.* ASPCA. https://www.aspca.org/pet-care/cat-care/common-cat-behavior-issues/meowing-and-yowling

2. Science Reference Section, Library of Congress. (n.d.). *Why and how do cats purr?* The Library of Congress. https://www.loc.gov/everyday-mysteries/zoology/item/why-and-how-do-cats-purr/

3. Leeson, J. (2023a, February 17). *5 reasons why cats hiss & How to Stop the behavior.* The Dog People by Rover.com. https://www.rover.com/blog/cat-hissing/

4. Hill's Pet Nutrition, Inc. (2022, August 30). *The Tales Your Cat's Tail Tells.* Hill's Pet Nutrition. https://www.hillspet.com/cat-care/behavior-appearance/cat-tail-language

5. Shojai, A. (2022, December 8). *Reasons why cats bite and how to stop it.* The Spruce Pets. https://www.thesprucepets.com/stop-cat-bites-553893

6. Copeland, K. (2024, January 2). *Why do cats blink slowly? their behavior explained.* Catster. https://www.catster.com/cat-behavior/why-do-cats-blink-slowly/

3

HEALTH AND WELLNESS: KEEPING YOUR KITTEN THRIVING

A cat's health is a reflection of the care it receives

— ANONYMOUS

I n this chapter, we will cover common health issues, emergencies, finding the right veterinarian, and meeting your kitten's nutritional needs. Additionally, we'll provide tips for creating a fun and stimulating environment for your kitten to prevent boredom and grumpiness. You'll learn how to identify health issues such as upper respiratory infections, intestinal parasites, fleas, and ticks, and how to choose safe and appropriate toys for playtime. We'll also discuss the importance of finding the right food for your kitten and stimulating their natural instincts. Lastly, we'll provide information on preparing for emergencies and finding the right vet. This is your ultimate guide to kitten health and wellness.

So, let's get started and show your kitten some love by keeping them healthy, happy, and entertained. Trust me, your kitten will love you even more for it (if that's even possible).

EARLY VETERINARIAN CARE

Early veterinary healthcare is a kitten's best shot at a longer and healthier life. Kittens should visit the vet every 3 to 4 weeks until they are about 4 months old.[1] These visits are essential for several reasons.

Firstly, kittens require a series of vaccinations to protect them against common infectious diseases such as feline viral rhinotracheitis, calicivirus, and panleukopenia.[2] These vaccines are typically given in a series over the first several months of a kitten's life. After that, regular veterinary visits ensure the vaccines are administered on time, and the kitten is protected against these diseases.

Secondly, regular veterinary visits allow the veterinarian to monitor the kitten's growth and development. Kittens grow rapidly, and any abnormalities or delays in growth can be detected early and addressed promptly. Additionally, early detection of any health issues can lead to more effective treatment and a better outcome for the kitten.

Finally, regular veterinary visits allow the veterinarian to educate kitten owners about proper nutrition, behavior, and parasite prevention. Kittens have different nutritional needs than adult cats, and a veterinarian can recommend an appropriate diet. Additionally, kittens require socialization and training to become well-behaved adult cats. Finally, regular preventive care, such as flea and tick prevention, is essential for a kitten's overall health.

CHOOSING THE RIGHT VETERINARIAN: FINDING THE PURRRFECT FIT

As a new kitten owner, choosing the right veterinarian is one of the most critical decisions to ensure your kitten's health and well-being. Your kitten's health will depend mainly on their quality of veterinary care.

When searching for a veterinarian, looking for one specializing in feline care and with experience with kitten health is essential. In addition, you want a vet with the technical skills to diagnose and treat any medical conditions your kitten may face and understand the unique needs and behavior of cats.

Ask for recommendations from other pet owners or your local animal shelter to find a good vet. These sources can provide valuable insights into the quality of care provided by different veterinarians in your area. Once you have a few names, scheduling a visit to meet with the vet before committing to their services is essential. This will allow you to see the facility, meet the staff, and ask questions.

In addition to having the proper credentials and experience, you want a veterinarian you feel comfortable communicating with. You should be able to discuss your kitten's health and any concerns you have openly and honestly with your vet without feeling rushed or dismissed. Look for a vet who is willing to take the time to answer all of your questions and who is genuinely interested in helping you keep your kitten healthy and happy.

Remember, your kitten's health is your responsibility as a pet owner, and finding the right veterinarian is a foundational step in providing the best possible care. Take the time to research and select a vet who you trust and who shares your commitment to your kitten's health and well-being. Your kitten will thank you for it!

FELINE HEALTH 101: FROM COMMON ISSUES TO EMERGENCY PREPAREDNESS

Even though you may have access to excellent veterinary care, learning about common health issues that kittens may experience is crucial for ensuring your kitten's health and well-being. Kittens are vulnerable to various health issues such as upper respiratory infections, intestinal parasites, fleas, and ticks, and early detection of these issues is key to successful treatment.

UPPER RESPIRATORY INFECTIONS (URI)

Upper respiratory infections (URI) are indeed one of the most common health issues that kittens face, and they can cause a range of symptoms such as sneezing, coughing, runny nose, and fever. Kittens are particularly susceptible to URI because their immune systems are still developing and have not been exposed to many viruses and bacteria.

If you suspect that your kitten has a URI, it's essential to take them to the veterinarian as soon as possible for a diagnosis and treatment. Depending on the severity of the infection, your veterinarian may prescribe antibiotics or other medications to help your kitten feel better.

In addition to seeking veterinary care, there are several things you can do to help your kitten recover from a URI. First, keep your kitten in a warm and comfortable environment, and ensure they have plenty of fresh water and nutritious food. You can also use a humidifier or steam to help relieve their congestion.

Prevention is key when it comes to URI in kittens. Keeping your kitten away from sick cats and vaccinating them can help reduce the risk of URI.

INTESTINAL PARASITES

Intestinal parasites are common for kittens and can cause symptoms such as vomiting, diarrhea, weight loss, and a bloated belly. Roundworms and tapeworms are two of the most common intestinal parasites in kittens.

If you suspect your kitten has an intestinal parasite, it's essential to take them to the veterinarian for a diagnosis and treatment. Your veterinarian can perform a fecal exam to determine the type of parasite present and prescribe the appropriate deworming medication to treat and prevent the recurrence of the parasite.

Prevention is also important when it comes to intestinal parasites. Keeping your kitten's living area clean and free of feces can help reduce the risk of infection. Additionally, regular veterinary check-ups and deworming treatments can help prevent intestinal parasites from becoming a problem in the first place.

Overall, it's important to stay vigilant regarding intestinal parasites in kittens. By seeking veterinary care at the first sign of symptoms and taking preventative measures, you can help keep your kitten healthy and happy.

FLEAS AND TICKS

Fleas and ticks are common external parasites that can cause various health problems for kittens, including itching, irritation, and skin infections. These parasites require blood from an animal host to live and reproduce and can persist in the environment.

Preventing flea and tick infestations in kittens is essential, and several prevention products are available on the market. Consulting with a veterinarian is vital in determining the best prevention product for your kitten, as different products have different active ingredients and dosages that are appropriate for different ages and weights of kittens. Some common flea and tick prevention products for kittens include topical treatments, oral medications, and collars.

- Topical treatments are usually applied to the back of the kitten's neck and are absorbed through the skin, providing protection against fleas and ticks for a limited time.
- Oral medications can also be given to kittens to protect against fleas and ticks, and some of these medications also protect against other parasites, such as heartworms and intestinal worms.

• Flea and tick collars are another option, and they
  release a chemical that repels fleas and ticks from
  your kitten's coat

EMERGENCY PREPAREDNESS: PLANNING FOR THE UNEXPECTED

In an emergency, having a plan in place is essential for the
safety and well-being of your kitten. Along with creating an
emergency kit, several other necessary steps are needed to
prepare for emergencies.

First and foremost, it's essential to have a pet first aid kit
readily available. According to the Centers for Disease Control
and Prevention, this kit should include bandages, antiseptic,
gauze, and any medications your kitten may require. Additionally, it's crucial to have important documents such as vaccination history, any existing health conditions, drugs, and contact
information for your veterinarian in an emergency.[3]

In addition to preparing a pet first aid kit, you must famil-
iarize yourself with common emergencies your kitten may
face. For example, choking and poisoning are common emergencies that can be life-threatening for your kitten. Knowing
how to respond in these situations can make all the difference
in saving your kitten's life.

CHOKING KITTEN PREPAREDNESS

Choking can be a scary and life-threatening situation for both
humans and kittens, and it's essential to know how to respond
quickly and effectively. In the case of choking, the first step is
to try to remove the object causing the blockage.

For pets, it's essential to approach the situation calmly and avoid startling or causing additional distress to the animal. If you can safely and quickly remove the object causing the blockage, do so immediately. Be careful not to push the object further down the animal's throat, which can cause further harm.

If you cannot remove the object causing the blockage, seek veterinary assistance immediately. Your veterinarian can perform life-saving measures, such as an emergency tracheostomy or endoscopy, to remove the object and restore proper breathing.

It's important to note that prevention is critical regarding choking for kittens. Avoid giving your pet small toys, bones, or other objects they can easily swallow. Always supervise your pet during playtime and mealtime, and take the necessary precautions to ensure their safety.

Remember, choking can happen at any time, and being prepared is essential.

KITTEN POISONING PREPAREDNESS

In the unfortunate event of poisoning, time is of the essence. Therefore, it's crucial to act quickly to minimize the effects of the poison and prevent further harm to your pet. If you suspect your kitten has been poisoned, it's essential to contact your veterinarian or a pet poison control hotline right away for guidance on how to proceed.

When you contact your veterinarian or poison control hotline, be sure to provide as much information as possible about the type of poison your pet has been exposed to, the amount ingested, and the time of ingestion. This information can help the veterinarian or poison control specialist determine the best course of action.

However, it's never advisable to induce vomiting in cats at home, as this can lead to more severe symptoms and potentially worsen the existing problem. If you suspect that your kitten has ingested a toxic substance, it's crucial to seek veterinary attention immediately for proper diagnosis and treatment.[4]

Prevention is the best strategy when it comes to poisoning. Be sure to keep all toxic substances out of reach of your pets, including household cleaners, medications, and poisonous plants. Regularly inspect your home and yard for potential hazards and promptly address any issues.

KITTEN CPR

Knowing how to administer CPR to your kitten can also be helpful in case of an emergency. CPR for kittens is similar to CPR for humans, but it's essential to learn the proper technique from a qualified instructor to ensure that you're performing it correctly and safely. It's important to note that most kittens and cats that get to the point of needing CPR will not survive.[5] However, it is still a valuable tool if it becomes necessary to give your kitten the best chance at survival. Every second counts in an emergency, and acting quickly and confidently can make all the difference.

KITTEN MEDIC READY

Congrats, now you're an honorary kitten medic! When it comes to emergencies, being prepared is half the battle. Don't let a crisis catch you off guard - create a pet first aid kit, keep essential documents handy, learn how to handle common emergencies, and master the art of kitty CPR. With these skills under your belt, you'll be ready to save the day. But that's not all - next up, we're diving into the world of kitten nutrition and setting them up for a lifetime of good health. So get ready to become a kitty nutrition pro!

FEEDING FELINES: FROM CARNIVOROUS ANCESTORS TO PICKY EATERS

Domestic cats are descended from African wildcats, primarily carnivorous hunters.[6] As cats evolved, their diet also evolved to meet their nutritional needs. Today, domestic cats are obligate carnivores, which means they require a diet that consists primarily of animal protein to survive and thrive. Understanding the evolutionary history of cats and their dietary needs can benefit cat owners in several ways. By providing a balanced and nutritious diet that mimics their natural diet, cat owners can help their cats maintain optimal health, including healthy skin and fur, strong muscles and bones, and a healthy immune system.

Additionally, a diet that meets their nutritional needs can help prevent health issues like obesity, diabetes, and kidney disease. By understanding domestic cats' natural diet and dietary requirements, cat owners can make informed choices when selecting the right food for their feline friends, ultimately contributing to their overall health and well-being. It can also help us understand why cats are such picky eaters.

A balanced and nutritious diet is essential for your kitten's growth and development. Choose a high-quality kitten food that meets the nutritional requirements for kittens, including protein, fat, and essential vitamins and minerals. Avoid feeding your kitten table scraps or human food, which can cause digestive problems and nutritional imbalances. Also, avoid cat food that contains fillers, artificial flavors or colors, and excessive amounts of carbohydrates. It's also important to feed your kitten the appropriate amount of food based on age and weight, as overfeeding can lead to obesity and other health problems.

YOU ARE WHAT YOU EAT: AVOIDING DRY

While dry kibble food may seem convenient and affordable, there are several reasons why it should be avoided for the sake of your kitten's health.

Firstly, dry food is inherently dehydrating. The low moisture content of dry food can lead to chronic dehydration, contributing to urinary tract disease and other health problems.

As we've already mentioned, cats are obligate carnivores, meaning their specialized diet has led to several physiological adaptations, including a low thirst drive and a reliance on obtaining most of their moisture intake from their food. In the wild, cats consume their whole prey, getting their water and nutritional needs from their food. While domesticated cats have their water readily available, they still retain the trait of obtaining most of their water from their food, which is why feeding them high-quality, moisture-rich food is crucial to their overall health and well-being.

When you provide your kitten with dry kibble, you are essentially depriving them of their primary source of moisture, which is something they have evolved to depend on. This can have severe consequences for their overall health and well-being.

In addition to dehydration, many dry foods are also high in carbohydrates. Cats require little to no carbohydrates in their diet, so a diet that is too high in carbohydrates can lead to weight gain and other health issues, such as diabetes.

Furthermore, dry food is heavily processed and often contains additives and preservatives that can be harmful to kittens. Some of these additives are added to improve the taste and appearance of the food rather than for any nutritional benefit.

Finally, it is essential to note that many dry food products are made with low-quality ingredients that do not provide the nutrients pets need. In addition, while some high-quality dry foods exist, many commercial brands contain fillers and by-products of little nutritional value.[7]

RAW OVER WET.

As I mentioned in Chapter 1, you are much better off going with wet food over dry kibble. While wet food is often considered a convenient and optimal middle ground between dry kibble and a raw diet, it is essential to note that a raw diet has many benefits that wet food simply cannot match.

A raw food diet closely resembles what cats would consume in the wild, consisting primarily of meat, bones, and organs. By feeding cats a raw diet, they can receive numerous health benefits, including healthier skin, a shiny coat, and improved digestion.

In contrast, most wet cat food undergoes some level of processing and may contain some of the same harmful ingredients that are commonly found in dry kibble. Therefore, while wet food can be a good source of hydration and may contain higher-quality ingredients than dry kibble, it is not a perfect solution.

Therefore, while wet food can be a good option for some cats, I want to encourage new kitten owners to be thinking about eventually transitioning to a raw diet. It is essential to acknowledge that no amount of food processing can fully replicate the experience of a cat in the wild, hunting, and feasting on a freshly caught prey animal. However, by choosing the best possible food options that mimic a natural diet, you can come closer to providing your kitten with the nutrition and experience they need to thrive.

So, if you're reading this and decide you want to provide only the best for your new companion, you may be wondering what the options are for you. Here are some of the most common:

- **Make your own raw cat food:** One option is to prepare your cat's raw food yourself. This involves sourcing high-quality ingredients, such as raw meat, bones, and organs, and preparing them safely and appropriately for your cat. It's important to note that preparing raw cat food at home requires some knowledge of feline nutrition and food safety, so it's a good idea to do your research or consult with a veterinarian or a veterinary nutritionist.
- **Buy pre-made raw cat food:** Another option is to purchase pre-made raw cat food from a pet food store or online retailer. Many companies now offer frozen or freeze-dried raw cat food that is formulated to meet feline nutritional requirements. These products can be more convenient than

making your own raw food but also more expensive.

- **Incorporate raw food into your cat's diet:** If you're not ready to switch your cat to a fully raw food diet, you can still incorporate some raw food into their meals. For example, you might add raw meat or organs as a topper to your cat's regular food or offer raw bones as a treat. This can provide some of the benefits of a raw food diet without fully committing to the lifestyle.

It's crucial to approach these options with caution. Raw food diets require a deep understanding of feline nutrition and food safety. It's essential to recognize that all of these options come with potential risks, so it's essential to do your research and make informed decisions about your cat's nutrition. By consulting with a veterinarian or a veterinary nutritionist and researching different brands and preparation methods, you can help ensure that you are providing your cat with the best possible nutrition in a safe and effective way.

Overall, if you are a kitten owner, a raw food diet for your furry companion is worth considering. While it may take some extra effort to prepare and serve, the health benefits are well worth it. Additionally, with the increasing availability of raw, freeze-dried food, it is becoming more accessible than ever to feed your kitten a nutritious diet.

BATHTUB BANDITS: WHY CATS PREFER RUNNING WATER

Finally, it's time to deliver on all those water fountain plugs I made in Chapter 1. Trust me, at the end of this section, you will

understand why this is one of the most important purchases you will make for your kitten. Cats have a unique preference for running water, which can be traced back to their ancestral roots as desert animals. In the wild, cats would hunt for their prey in the dry, arid terrain of the desert, and as already mentioned they obtained most of their moisture intake through their food. As a result, they have evolved to be highly efficient at conserving water and have developed an instinctual preference for running water over stagnant water.[8]

Investing in a cat water fountain can be an excellent way to provide your kitten with fresh, running water that mimics their natural environment in the wild. A cat water fountain can also help encourage your kitten to drink more water, as running water sounds more enticing and appealing to them than a stagnant water bowl.

Additionally, many cats are drawn to bathtubs and sinks because of the running water they provide. The sound of running water can be soothing to cats and trigger their natural instinct to drink. Some cats even enjoy playing with the running water, pawing at it, or attempting to catch it.

By providing your kitten with fresh, running water through a cat water fountain, you can help ensure they stay hydrated and healthy. And, if your kitten is one of those water-loving felines, you may want to keep an eye on them the next time you turn on the faucet – you never know what kind of bathtub or sink hijinks they might get up to!

However, while it's essential to invest in a cat water fountain to meet your kitten's unique preference for running water, it's equally important to maintain and clean the fountain regularly to ensure the water is safe and appealing for your kitten to drink. Cats can be sensitive to the buildup of bacteria and other contaminants in their water. As a result, a dirty water fountain can lead to health problems or discourage your kitten from drinking from it altogether.

Many cat water fountains are designed for easy cleaning, with dishwasher-safe components or simple disassembly for cleaning. It's recommended to clean your cat water fountain at least once a week, but more frequent cleaning may be necessary if you have multiple cats or if the fountain is used frequently.

In addition to being easy to clean, many cat water fountains include charcoal filters to help purify and improve the taste of the water. These filters can help remove impurities, such as hair and debris, and absorb unpleasant tastes or odors from the water source. It's essential to replace these filters regularly, as the manufacturer recommends, to ensure that they continue to work effectively. By regularly cleaning and maintaining your cat water fountain and replacing the charcoal filters as needed, you can provide your kitten with fresh, clean, and delicious water at all times.

TREATS

Treats can be a great way to bond with your kitten, provide additional nutrition, and reward them for good behavior. However, choosing treats formulated explicitly for kittens ensures they get the appropriate nutrients and portion sizes. Treats intended for adult cats or dogs may contain ingredients that are not appropriate for kittens, and the portion sizes may be too large for their tiny stomachs.

Kitten treats come in various flavors and textures, from soft and chewy to crunchy and biscuit-like. Some treats contain additional nutrients, such as vitamins and minerals, to support your kitten's growth and development. When selecting treats for your kitten, it's essential to read the label carefully to ensure the ingredients are safe and appropriate for their age and size.

While treats can provide additional nutrition and bonding opportunities, avoiding overfeeding is essential. Treats should make up no more than 10% of your kitten's daily calorie intake,[9] and it's important to adjust their regular meals accordingly to avoid overfeeding and potential weight gain. In addition, overfeeding can lead to health problems such as obesity, diabetes, and other health issues.

NAVIGATING DIETARY RESTRICTIONS AND ALLERGIES FOR YOUR KITTEN

By the time you realize your kitten has a food allergy, they may already be a full-grown cat. However, some kittens could show signs of a food allergy early in their kitten-hood. The most common symptoms of food allergies in cats are constant itching and scratching, which can lead to secondary infections and sores. Food allergies can also cause gastrointestinal upset, such as diarrhea and vomiting.

Believe it or not, food allergies in cats are rare. Only around 1% of all cats have food allergies, but that number jumps to 15% for cats with itchy skin. And - if a cat has itchy skin and gastrointestinal symptoms, up to 42% of them could suffer from food allergies.[10]

Common cat allergens include beef, dairy, and fish, although food allergies can be caused by any food substance. If you suspect your kitten has a food allergy, taking prompt action and seeking veterinary care is essential.

The standard method for diagnosis is to put your kitty on a strict hypoallergenic diet for 8 to 12 weeks to see if their symptoms improve. If they do, you can reintroduce their old food to see if symptoms return. If they do, it's back to the hypoallergenic food for your feline friend. Then, you can start introducing individual ingredients every 2 weeks to see if they worsen their symptoms. If none do, your cat is in the clear!

When it comes to treatment, the key is to avoid any ingredients that could trigger an allergic reaction. Prescription diets are a good choice for hypoallergenic food trials because they're held to higher quality control standards than over-the-counter cat food, which can contain contaminants that set off allergies. Just be aware that it can take up to 10 weeks for symptoms to completely go away and that strict dietary management will be necessary to keep your cat healthy and happy.

GROOMING AND HANDLING

Taking care of your kitten's physical needs is essential to their overall well-being. Grooming and handling are two critical aspects of physical care that cat owners need to pay attention to. To ensure that your kitten is comfortable with grooming and handling, use positive reinforcement early. This will help prevent fear and anxiety associated with grooming and handling and make trips to the vet less stressful.

HOW TO HANDLE YOUR KITTEN

The scruff refers to the loose skin at the back of a cat or kitten's neck, between their shoulder blades. This area of skin is different from the rest of the cat's skin because it is not attached to any muscles or bones.[11] Picking up a kitten by the scruff is a technique commonly used by mother cats to move their young from place to place. While it is generally safe to pick up a young kitten by the scruff of the neck, it is vital to do so with care and for only short periods of time.

The scruffing technique involves grasping the kitten's neck skin between your thumb and fingers and lifting them up. When done correctly, the kitten should remain relaxed and calm, as if they were being carried by their mother. However, if done improperly or too long, the kitten may become uncomfortable or experience pain.

It is important to note that the scruffing technique should only be used for young kittens, typically those under eight weeks old. As kittens grow and their neck muscles develop, the scruffing approach becomes less effective and can even cause harm to the animal. Therefore, it is best for older kittens or cats to support their body with your hands and avoid using the scruffing technique.

GROOMING YOUR KITTEN

Cats groom each other as a sign of affection and bonding, which is called allogrooming. Allogrooming is a way for cats to strengthen social bonds and communicate with each other using pheromones. For cat owners, grooming their cats can also help them bond with their pets and maintain their cats' coats and skin health by removing dirt and debris, distributing natural oils, and preventing matting. It also allows you to check for any skin issues or abnormalities. Depending on your kitten's coat, you may need to brush them daily or a few times a week.

Start with short, positive sessions of handling and grooming, gradually increasing the length and intensity as your kitten becomes more comfortable. Start by introducing a soft brush and slowly work up to using a slicker brush or comb. Use treats and praise to encourage good behavior, make the experience more enjoyable, and build a bond between you and your kitten.

Trimming your kitten's nails is also essential to prevent them from scratching and damaging furniture or hurting themselves. Begin by getting your kitten used to having their paws touched and massaged. This can be done during grooming or handling sessions. Once your kitten is comfortable, introduce nail trimming using specially designed cat nail clippers. Make sure to only trim the tips and avoid the quick, which is the pink area of the nail that contains blood vessels and nerves. If the quick is cut, it can result in severe pain and bleeding, which can be a scary experience for you and your kitten.

BATHING

While humans often need a bath or shower to stay clean and healthy, cats rely on their tongues and paws to keep themselves tidy. One of the primary reasons why cats spend so much time grooming is to remove dirt and parasites from their fur. In the wild, cats would need to hunt and protect themselves from predators, and being dirty could make them more vulnerable. Moreover, grooming is vital to maintaining their body temperature, especially during hot weather. Cats spread saliva by licking themselves over their fur, which helps evaporate and cool them down.[12]

Cats' tongues have unique features that make grooming efficient and effective. Their tongues are covered with tiny barbs called papillae that point backward, making removing loose hair and debris from their fur easier. The papillae also help cats to distribute their natural oils, which keeps their coat shiny and healthy.

Because of this, most cats are self-sufficient when it comes to grooming. It's sometimes hard for new kitten parents to understand this, especially if they are used to grooming dogs, but kittens and cats almost treat it like a second job. They know how to keep themselves clean and usually do not require further help.

However, Cats with skin allergies, flea infestations, or other medical conditions may require some help bathing to keep them clean and healthy. If you choose to bathe your kitten, it requires special attention and care, as cats may become stressed and agitated. Use a mild shampoo formulated specifically for kittens to bathe a cat safely. If possible, use a shower or sink hose to concentrate the water directly on the kitten while using warm water that is not too hot or cold. Avoid getting water in their ears and eyes, and limit bathing to when necessary. Overbathing a cat can remove essential oils from its coat and cause dry skin.

PHYSICAL AND MENTAL WELL-BEING: HONING YOUR KITTEN'S INNER PREDATOR

Kittens are born hunters and love to chase and catch prey. To bring out your kitten's inner hunter, you can make mealtime a little more exciting by moving their food around and making them work for it. When I first started doing this with Mouse, it was amazing to see how she reacted to this simple change - she became more engaged and focused and seemed to enjoy her food more when she had to work for it.

Another way to stimulate your kitten's natural instincts is by hiding treats around the house and watching them go on a little treasure hunt. It's fun for them and a great way to provide them with mental and physical stimulation. Starting with accessible hiding spots and gradually making it more challenging helps keep them engaged and interested while giving a sense of accomplishment when they find the treats.

In addition to these activities, giving your kitten plenty of playtime and exercise is essential. This can be interactive play with toys or just running around and playing with them. Providing a variety of toys to keep them interested and engaged, such as balls, mice, and interactive toys, is also helpful.

Stimulating your kitten's natural instincts through these types of activities not only provides them with mental and physical stimulation and helps prevent boredom and destructive behavior.[13] For example, you may notice that when your kitten is engaged in natural hunting behaviors, they are less likely to scratch your furniture or chew on household objects.

CONCLUSION

Taking care of your kitten's health and wellness is no small feat, but it's vital if you want them to grow up to be healthy and happy cats. To achieve that, you gotta pay attention to a few things like understanding common health issues, preparing for emergencies, finding the right veterinarian, and providing proper nutrition. Trust me, your kitten will thank you for it.

Alright, that's it for now. In the next chapter, we'll dive into litter box training to help you maintain your kitten's hygiene and cleanliness and prevent accidents. So, stay tuned, and let's keep those kittens happy and healthy!

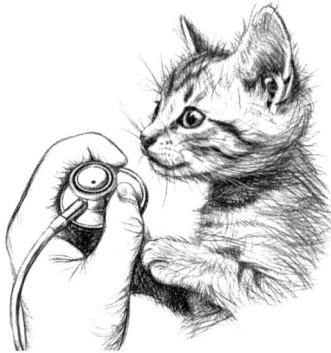

1. Bukowski, J. A., & Aiello, S. (2023, December 5). *Routine health care of cats.* Merck Veterinary Manual. https://www.merckvetmanual.com/cat-owners/routine-care-and-breeding-of-cats/routine-health-care-of-cats
2. Grzyb, K., DVM. (2023, December 6). *Kitten vaccination schedule and costs.* PetMD. https://www.petmd.com/cat/general-health/kitten-vaccination-schedule-and-costs
3. Centers for Disease Control and Prevention, National Center for Emerging and Zoonotic Infectious Diseases (NCEZID). (2022, September 14). *Pet*

Safety in Emergencies. cdc.gov. https://www.cdc.gov/healthypets/keeping-pets-and-people-healthy/emergencies.html

4. Morrison, B. J., DVM. (2023, September 12). *Poisons in cats.* PetMD. https://www.petmd.com/cat/poisoning/poisons-in-cats

5. PetMD Editorial. (2022, August 11). *CPR for Cats and Kittens.* Video and Article | PetMD. https://www.petmd.com/cat/emergency/common-emergencies/e_ct_respiration_cpr

6. Team Africa Geographic. (2021, July 26). *African wildcat.* Africa Geographic. https://africageographic.com/stories/african-wildcat/

7. Hofve, J., DVM. (2023, January 20). *10 reasons why dry food is bad for cats & dogs | Little Big Cat - Dr. Jean Hofve.* Little Big Cat - Dr. Jean Hofve. https://littlebigcat.com/why-dry-food-is-bad-for-cats-and-dogs/

8. Smithsonian's National Zoo and Conservation Biology Institute. (n.d.). *Sand cat.* https://nationalzoo.si.edu/animals/sand-cat

9. Fields, L. (2017, February 15). *The right way to treat your pet.* WebMD. https://pets.webmd.com/pet-treats

10. Burkett, L., DVM. (2023, September 20). *Food allergies in cats.* PetMD. https://www.petmd.com/cat/conditions/digestive/food-allergies-cats

11. Elliott, P., Mrcvs. (2023, August 9). *6 ways to handle a cat - WikiHow.* wiki-How. https://www.wikihow.com/Handle-a-Cat

12. Naser, N. (2023, August 9). *Why do cats lick themselves when grooming?* BeChewy. https://be.chewy.com/why-do-cats-lick-themselves-when-grooming/

13. Boicelli, C. (2023, May 23). *Cat enrichment: What to do if your cat is bored.* https://www.preventivevet.com/cats/cat-enrichment-for-bored-cats

4

THE SCOOP ON LITTER TRAINING

The phrase 'domestic cat' is an oxymoron

— GEORGE F. WILL

After bringing home our first kitten, Mouse, we discovered that she had a bit of a problem with using the litter box. Instead of using it, she would always make a beeline for any brown paper grocery bag we had lying around and swiftly do her business in there. It was like she thought she was in a safe, cozy cave or something.

Initially, I was puzzled because I had always assumed that cats had an inherent ability to use the litter box, so I tried to reprimand her as one would a disobedient puppy. However, my disciplinary actions proved to be ineffective, as I later discovered through research that cats do not respond well to this kind of discipline. Rather, such treatment could confuse them and damage the human-cat bond because they associate the negative treatment with you, not their actions. Realizing that our disciplinary actions merely perplexed her, my wife, Megan, and I decided to change our approach. We opted to wait patiently for Mouse to learn how to use the litter box on her own, understanding that positive reinforcement was a more effective means of instruction for cats.

And boy, did we ever give her some affirmation when she finally did! We both rushed to the litter box, cheering and clapping and telling her what a good kitty she was. I'm pretty sure our neighbors must have thought we were weird with all the noise we were making.

But you know what? It worked! Mouse started using the litter box on her own, and we didn't have to worry about more surprise presents in brown paper bags. So now, it's time to tackle one of the biggest challenges of owning a kitten – litter box training.

THE EVOLUTION OF CAT LITTER

Cats are natural-born predators and have an innate tendency to bury their waste to avoid detection by other predators. This instinct makes them inclined to use a litter box as it provides them with a suitable area to eliminate their waste.

The history of cats using litter boxes can be traced back to the 1950s when new kinds of clay led to the development of the modern cat litter. Before the introduction of cat litter, most people fed their cats table scraps, bread, and of course, cream, which led to unpleasant smells emanating from the litter box.[1]

In 1961, the brand Cat's Pride® Cat Litter was introduced to the pet care market, revolutionizing how cats relieved themselves indoors. Cat owners no longer had to rely on dirt or sand as makeshift litter, and the use of litter boxes became more widespread.

Over the years, cat litter has undergone several improvements, such as the development of clumping litter in the 1980s, which made it easier to scoop and clean litter boxes. Today, cat litter comes in various materials, including clay, silica gel, recycled paper, and natural materials like pine and wheat.

In this comprehensive chapter, I will guide you through the essential steps of providing a comfortable and hygienic environment for your feline friend. We'll begin by discussing how to select the perfect litter box that meets your cat's needs, followed by the importance of choosing a suitable litter to suit your cat's preferences and your own environmental and health convictions. We'll then delve into the vital aspect of training your kitten to use the litter box, sharing expert tips on avoiding accidents and maintaining a spotless litter box. By the end of this chapter, you'll have all the knowledge and confidence to provide your furry companion with a clean and comfortable space to meet their natural needs.

CHOOSING THE RIGHT LITTER BOX FOR YOUR KITTEN

Choosing the right size litter box is crucial for your kitten's comfort and well-being. When deciding on the size, consider your kitten's age and size. A litter box that is too small can be difficult for your kitten to use, leading to accidents or avoidance. In contrast, a litter box that is too large can be challenging for your kitten to enter and exit. According to the (n+1) rule, it's generally recommended to have one more litter box than the number of cats you have. Therefore, if you have one kitten, consider having two litter boxes. If you have two kittens, consider having three litter boxes. That way, your kitten has a backup option if one is unavailable or already in use. Your kitten (and your carpet) will thank you for it!

COVERED OR UNCOVERED?

When choosing the perfect litter box for your kitten, size isn't the only thing to consider. Covered and uncovered litter boxes can also play a role in your kitten's preference. Covered litter boxes may offer privacy and reduce litter scatter and odor, which can be a real plus for cat owners. However, it's important to note that not all cats are fans of covered litter boxes. In fact, a study found that only 15% of cats used the covered box more than the uncovered one, while 70% showed no preference at all.[2]

Some cats may feel trapped or confined in a covered litter box, which can cause them to avoid using it. So, if you decide to use a covered litter box, ensure there is enough room for your kitten to move around comfortably. Also, be sure to keep the litter box clean and well-maintained to prevent odors and encourage your kitten to use it.

To help keep the area clean, consider using a litter mat. A litter mat is designed to catch excess litter that may have gotten stuck to your kitten's paws when they exit the litter box. It's a great way to prevent litter from being tracked outside the box and making a mess around your home.

Ultimately, choosing a covered or uncovered litter box depends on your kitten's preferences. Keep in mind that cats tend to think inside the box - as long as it's clean and comfortable. So, take the time to observe your kitten's behavior and preferences, and choose a litter box that meets their needs.

SELF-CLEANING?

Convenience is definitely a factor to consider when choosing the right litter box. Self-cleaning litter boxes are a popular option for busy cat owners, as they can save time and effort when it comes to scooping and cleaning the litter box. However, they may not be the best choice for every kitten, especially those who are timid or easily frightened.

The noise and movement of a self-cleaning litter box can be overwhelming for some kittens, causing them to feel anxious or scared. This can lead to litter box avoidance or even accidents outside the litter box. On the other hand, suppose your kitten is timid or easily frightened. In that case, opt for a traditional litter box until they become more comfortable with the routine and the sounds associated with a self-cleaning litter box.

THE LITTER

Until now, we've been discussing the litter box itself, but it's imperative to shift our attention toward the crucial component that fills it: the litter. With so many types of litter on the market, knowing which is best for your kitten can be challenging. This section will provide an overview of the different types of cat litter and their pros and cons to help you make an informed decision.

CLAY LITTER

Clay litter is popular among cat owners due to its affordability and convenience. It comes in two primary forms: clumping and non-clumping. Clumping clay litter forms lumps when the cat urinates, making it easy to scoop out and dispose of the waste. On the other hand, non-clumping clay litter is known for its excellent odor-absorbing properties, making it an ideal choice for cat owners who prioritize odor control. However, it's important to note that clay litter can have some downsides. It is often dusty and heavy, creating a mess around the litter box and potentially affecting air quality. Additionally, clay litter is not biodegradable, which can contribute to environmental pollution when disposed of in landfills (more on this later).

CRYSTAL LITTER

Another popular litter option is Crystal litters, made from silica gel. They are popular among cat owners due to their high absorbency and longer lifespan. The crystals quickly absorb urine and trap odors, keeping the litter box smelling fresh for longer periods. Additionally, crystal litter is known to track less than other types of litter, making it easier to clean up after your feline friend. One of the most significant advantages of crystal litter is that it requires less frequent scooping than other types of litter, reducing the time and effort needed to maintain the litter box.

However, it's worth noting that crystal litter can be relatively expensive compared to other types of litter.

NATURAL LITTERS

Environmentally minded cat owners point out that many traditional cat litters are made from non-renewable materials, such as clay and silica, which require significant energy to mine and transport. In addition, once used, cat litter is typically disposed of in landfills, where it can take years to decompose and can contribute to environmental pollution. Because of this, natural litters have become a popular choice among cat owners.

One of the advantages of natural litters is that they are made from renewable resources and are often biodegradable. This means they can break down and decompose naturally over time, benefiting the environment. Additionally, many natural litters are free from harsh chemicals and fragrances, making them a safer and healthier option for cats. Some common natural alternative litters include wood shaving, pine, paper, corn, wheat, walnut shell, and grass.[3]

However, there are some downsides to using natural litters. Each kind will have their own unique set of pros and cons, but generally speaking, some of the main concerns are that they may not be as absorbent as other types of litter. This means they may need to be changed more frequently to avoid odors and reduce the risk of bacterial growth. Additionally, natural litters may be more challenging to scoop than other types of litter, making cleaning the litter box more difficult.

When considering a natural litter, selecting one appropriate for your cat's needs and preferences is essential. For example, some cats may not like the texture or scent of certain types of natural litter. It's also important to keep in mind that natural litters can vary in quality and effectiveness depending on the brand and the specific material used.

TEACHING YOUR KITTEN TO USE THE LITTER BOX

Most kittens instinctively know how to use the litter box, but some may need extra help. Positive reinforcement is the best way to teach your kitten to use the litter box.

Start by placing your kitten in the litter box after meals and playtime. Encourage your kitten to dig in the litter with their paws. If your kitten uses the litter box successfully, reward them with a treat or praise. This will help your kitten associate the litter box with positive experiences.

As I mentioned before with our experience training Mouse, If your kitten has accidents outside the litter box, don't punish them. Punishment can cause your kitten to become fearful or anxious and may make litter box training more challenging. Just keep in mind that they also simply don't understand **"why"** you are punishing them, making the punishment useless to achieve the goal of behavior correction. Instead, clean up the mess and place your kitten back in the litter box. If your kitten continues to have accidents, it may be a sign of a medical issue, and you should consult your veterinarian.

MAINTAINING A CLEAN AND ODOR-FREE LITTER BOX

Maintaining a clean and odor-free litter box is crucial for your kitten's overall health and well-being. A dirty litter box can cause your kitten to avoid using it, leading to litter box aversion and inappropriate elimination in other areas of your home. This can be a frustrating and challenging problem to solve, so keeping the litter box clean is essential to avoid this issue.

Aside from affecting your kitten's behavior, a dirty litter box can also pose health risks to you and your kitten. The buildup of bacteria and ammonia from urine and feces can cause respiratory problems, such as asthma or bronchitis, in humans and cats. A dirty litter box can also attract flies, rodents, and other pests that can spread disease and make your home unsanitary. Therefore, It's crucial to scoop out waste and clumps daily. In addition, it's essential to replace the litter regularly to maintain a healthy and hygienic environment for your kitten.

In addition to daily scooping, it's essential to completely empty the litter box and wash it with unscented soap and water at least once a week. Using harsh chemicals or cleaners can be toxic to your kitten, so it's essential to use a mild soap that won't cause any harm.

CONCLUSION

So, what have we learned from this chapter? First and foremost, choosing the right litter box and litter is essential for your kitten's comfort and well-being. Positive reinforcement is the key to litter box training success, and punishment should be avoided. Finally, maintaining a clean and odor-free litter box is essential for your kitten's health and your own. We've also explored the benefits of using various natural litters as an eco-friendly alternative to traditional cat litter.

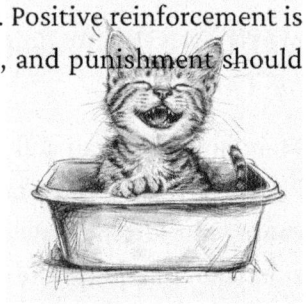

In Chapter 5, we'll dive into the world of kitten training and discipline, including understanding the benefits of training, teaching basic commands, and introducing fun tricks. We'll also discuss common behavior issues in kittens and provide tips for preventing destructive behavior like scratching and biting through positive reinforcement. So, get ready to become a pro at training and discipline!

1. Wilde, L. M. (2018, July 18). *The History of cat Litter and litter boxes | Cat Wisdom 101*. Cat Wisdom 101 | Everything Feline Since 2011. https://catwisdom101.com/history-cat-litter-litter-boxes/

2. Ward, E., Dr. (n.d.). *Covered or uncovered litter boxes: Do cats really care?* Pet Health Network. https://www.pethealthnetwork.com/cat-health/cat-behavior/covered-or-uncovered-litter-boxes-do-cats-really-care

3. Kruzer, A. (2021, September 16). *Eight different types of cat litter.* The Spruce Pets. https://www.thesprucepets.com/different-types-of-cat-litter-4688913

MAKE A DIFFERENCE WITH YOUR REVIEW: UNLOCK THE POWER OF GENEROSITY

Hey there, awesome readers!

Did you know that when you give just because you can, you're actually making your own life brighter? That's right, being generous not only feels good, but it might even help you live a happier and more prosperous life. And hey, if there's a chance to spread a little sunshine, let's grab it with both paws!

So, here's a little something I'm wondering...

Would you be willing to lend a paw to someone you've never met, without expecting a single treat in return?

Who might this mystery person be? Well, they're a lot like you were once—eager, full of curiosity about kittens, and ready to make a difference, but not quite sure how to start.

Our big dream is to make [taking care of kittens and cats] something anyone can do, no matter where they are. Everything I do—every word I write—is about helping that dream come true. But to make it happen, we need to reach out and touch every potential cat lover out there.

This is where you, my fellow kitten enthusiast, come in. Believe it or not, a lot of folks decide which book to cuddle up with based on what other readers say. So I'm reaching out to you on behalf of a [prospective kitten owner] somewhere out there:

Could you share a little bit of love by writing a review for this book?

It won't cost you a dime, and it'll only take a minute of your time. But your words could be the nudge that helps someone else make a furry friend's life better. Imagine your review helping...

...a local pet shop keep its doors open.

...a new cat parent feel less overwhelmed.

...a hardworking volunteer at a cat shelter find the perfect advice.

...an anxious kitty feel more at home.

...another cat dream come true.

Feeling that warm, fuzzy feeling inside? That's the joy of helping! And it's as easy as leaving a review. Just one minute, and you're done:

leave a review.

Scan or click the QR code below and tell the world what you think!

SCAN ME

If the thought of helping out a fellow kitten lover makes

you purr with happiness, then you're definitely our kind of person. Welcome to the club. You're one of the good ones.

I can't wait to show you how to make your bond with your kitty even stronger. You're going to love the tips and tricks waiting for you in the next chapters.

A huge thank you and a kitty high-five. Now, let's jump back into the whisker-licking good stuff.

• Your biggest fan, Julian Nivelles

P.S. - Did you know? When you share something helpful with someone, they'll remember you for it. If you think this book is the cat's meow and can help another [prospective kitten owner], why not spread the love and recommend it to them?

5

KITTEN BOOT CAMP: TRAINING AND DISCIPLINE

> You see, Greg, when you yell at a dog, his tail will go between his legs and cover his genitals, his ears will go down. A dog is very easy to break, but cats make you work for their affection. They don't sell out the way dogs do
>
> — JACK BYRNES

N ow that you have prepared your home established a bond with your kitten, and ensured their health and wellness, it's time to move on to training and discipline. This chapter will help you understand the benefits of training your kitten, teaching basic commands and tricks, and preventing unwanted behaviors.

As a cat parent, you might think training your kitten is unnecessary, but it can make a huge difference in their happiness, well-being and fulfillment. In this chapter, we'll explore the benefits of training your kitten, show you how to teach them basic commands and fun tricks, and give you tips for preventing and correcting destructive behaviors.

THE BENEFITS OF TRAINING YOUR KITTEN

Kittens are incredibly intelligent and curious creatures. You can help satisfy their need for mental stimulation and physical activity by training them. Additionally, training your kitten can help strengthen the bond between you and your furry friend. Here are some benefits of training your kitten:

- Training your kitten involves spending quality time with them, which can help deepen the bond between you and your kitten.
- Training can help prevent boredom and lethargy, leading to weight gain and other health issues.
- Training can help address behavior issues before they become a bigger problem.

THE FUTILITY OF DISCIPLINE

This statement may sound like a contradiction to the title of this chapter, but I promise it will make sense later. As discussed in earlier chapters, it is technically impossible to "discipline" your kitten. When it comes to cats and discipline, it's essential to understand that cats don't really understand the concept of discipline like dogs or humans do. In fact, trying to discipline a cat is often futile and not likely to yield the desired results.[1]

Cats are independent creatures who are more likely to respond to positive reinforcement rather than punishment. This means rewarding good behavior is a more effective way of encouraging your cat to repeat that behavior than punishing them for bad behavior. For example, if your cat scratches the designated scratching post instead of your furniture, rewarding them with treats or affection will reinforce that behavior and encourage them to continue using it.

It's important to remember that cats are not trying to misbehave or disobey us. They simply have their own instincts and needs that they are trying to fulfill. Understanding and meeting those needs, such as providing adequate playtime and scratching posts, is a more effective way of preventing unwanted behaviors than trying to discipline them. Therefore, when we say **"discipline,"** what we really mean is to influence and modify a kitten's behavior through positive reinforcement.

PREVENTING DESTRUCTIVE BEHAVIORS

Scratching furniture, counter surfing, and biting are some of the most common misbehaviors seen in kittens. Even though these behaviors may seem totally different, they all require the same two-step process to address and train your kitten. It's pretty simple, really. The first step is to understand why your kitten is doing these things. Once you have a handle on that, the second step is to make the behavior unappealing to your kitten and redirect their attention to something more appropriate. You can help your kitten learn to behave like a pro with a little effort and consistency!

For example, the first step to understanding why kittens engage in these behaviors:

- Scratching is a natural behavior for kittens as it helps them to mark their territory, stretch their muscles and sharpen their claws.
- Counter-surfing is common in kittens who like to perch because it allows them to observe their surroundings, feel secure, and satisfy their innate curiosity, much like their wildcat ancestors, who would climb trees to escape predators and hunt prey from an elevated vantage point.
- Biting can occur for various reasons, such as overstimulation or play aggression.

The next step is taking that information and making the behavior unappealing to the kitten and redirecting their attention to a more acceptable behavior that satisfies their needs:

- **Scratching furniture**: To curb this undesirable behavior, cat owners can make their furniture less appealing to cats by utilizing several effective methods, such as covering furniture with double-sided tape or using deterrent sprays and anti-scratch protectors. In addition to these tactics, providing cats with alternative scratching surfaces, like scratching posts or pads, and incentivizing their use through positive reinforcement, can effectively redirect their scratching behavior.

- **Counter surfing:** Discouraging counter surfing by cats can be achieved by making the counters unappealing to them, such as using double-sided tape or placing items on the counter, such as aluminum foil, that create noise if the cat jumps on them. Additionally, products, such as automatic air sprayers, can detect and deter cats by hitting them with a safe burst of air. Furthermore, providing cats with a designated elevated space, such as a cat tree, can reduce the likelihood of jumping on counters to satisfy their perching instincts and enable them to observe their surroundings without being in the midst of the action.
- **Biting:** To discourage biting, owners should redirect the cat's attention to a toy or other appropriate play item when they start to bite. It is important not to punish the cat for biting, as this can lead to fear and aggression. Instead, owners should reward positive behavior and ignore negative behavior.

The one critical constant you may or may not have noticed is that in all the examples of deterrence methods, the deterrent is never the human; it's always an object apart from the human like double-sided tape, foil, or various other products.

One common mistake cat owners make when trying to discourage bad behavior is using themselves as a negative consequence. For example, suppose the cat owner sprays the cat with water or physically moves them. In that case, this will cause the cat to associate the negative consequence with their owner rather than the behavior itself. This can lead to a breakdown in the cat-owner relationship and make it more challenging to train the cat in the future.

Instead of using ourselves as the negative consequence, using objects or deterrents that the cat can associate with the undesirable behavior is essential. This way, the deterrent is independent of the human, and therefore the cat will associate the negative consequence with the couch or countertops themselves and not the human.

COMMANDS AND TRICKS

Teaching your kitten basic commands and fun tricks can be a great way to bond with them while also providing mental stimulation and building their confidence. With patience and consistency, you can teach your kitten various skills to make your life together more enjoyable.

BASIC COMMANDS

To teach your kitten basic commands like sit, stay, and come, you can use a clicker and a treat to encourage them to perform the desired behavior. For example, to teach your kitten to sit, hold a treat in front of its nose and slowly move it up and over its head. As they follow the treat, their natural response will be to sit down. As soon as their bottom hits the ground, click the clicker and give them the treat.[2] Once your kitten has mastered the behavior, you can gradually phase out the clicker and the treats.

Fun tricks like high-five and roll-over are not only enjoyable for you and your kitten, but they also provide mental stimulation. To teach your kitten these tricks, use treats and positive reinforcement to encourage them to perform the trick. For example, to teach your kitten to high-five, hold a treat in front of their nose and then raise your hand slightly. As your kitten reaches for the treat, lift your hand up so they raise their paw. As soon as their paw touches your hand, click the clicker and give them the treat.

LEASH TRAINING

Leash training can be an excellent way to provide your kitten with safe outdoor time while also building a stronger bond with them. To start leash training, introduce your kitten to a harness and leash indoors, allowing them to explore the new sensation at their own pace. As they become more comfortable wearing the harness, you can gradually move outdoors and begin practicing walking on the leash. Patience and positive reinforcement are key when it comes to leash training, so be sure to offer plenty of treats and praise as your kitten progresses.

THAT'S SO FETCH!

Playing fetch is a fun and interactive activity that many cats enjoy. It can also help strengthen the bond between you and your kitten. While not all cats are natural fetch players, teaching your kitten to play fetch is a relatively simple process.

To start, you'll need a small toy or ball that your kitten can easily carry in their mouth. Encourage your kitten to chase after the toy by tossing it a short distance away. You can use a variety of toys, such as small stuffed animals, crinkly balls, or even wadded-up pieces of paper.

When your kitten picks up the toy and brings it back to you, offer plenty of praise and a treat as a reward. You may need to hold out your hand as a target for your kitten to return the toy to at first. Over time, your kitten may learn to retrieve the toy on their own and bring it back to you without prompting.[3]

As your kitten becomes more comfortable with the game, you can gradually increase the distance of the toss and even incorporate obstacles for them to navigate around. However, it's important to always supervise your kitten during playtime and never force them to play fetch if they seem disinterested or uncomfortable.

Remember to keep training sessions short and positive and practice in various environments to help your kitten generalize the behavior. You and your kitten can learn and grow together with patience, consistency, and positive reinforcement.

CREATING A ROUTINE FOR YOUR KITTEN

While it may seem like cats are nocturnal due to their tendency to be active at night, this is not actually the case. Cats are crepuscular animals, meaning that they are most active during dawn and dusk when their natural hunting instincts are triggered by the increased activity of prey animals.[4] Understanding a cat's circadian rhythm and natural behavior can help establish a routine that works well for you and your kitten. By scheduling playtime and feeding times around your cat's natural activity cycle, you can help them stay healthy and happy while also minimizing disruptive behavior during nighttime hours.

Here are some specific tips and tricks:

- **Feed your cat according to their natural schedule**: Since cats are most active during dawn and dusk, it's best to feed them during these times. Try to establish a consistent feeding schedule based on this natural rhythm. You can also use automatic feeders to ensure your cat always has access to food, even when you're not home.
- **Provide plenty of playtime during the day**: Even though cats are less active during the day, they still need mental and physical stimulation. So provide plenty of playtime and interactive toys during the day to keep your cat entertained and engaged.
- **Establish a consistent bedtime routine**: Cats thrive on routine, so it's crucial to establish a consistent bedtime routine to help them wind down and prepare for sleep. This can include a quiet play session, followed by a snack or a grooming session.
- **Provide a comfortable sleep environment**: Since cats are most active at night, providing a comfortable sleep environment is crucial to help them get the rest they need during the day. Ensure your cat has a comfortable bed in a quiet, dark room, away from distractions or disturbances.
- **Use natural light to regulate their internal clock**: Natural light is an essential cue for regulating a cat's internal clock. So provide plenty of natural light during the day, and dim the lights in the evening to help your cat prepare for sleep.

Having a routine is essential for kitten as it can help them feel more secure and relaxed in their environment. By establishing a consistent schedule for feeding, playtime, and sleep, you can help regulate your kitten's internal clock and promote a sense of stability. Additionally, having a set routine can make detecting changes in your kitten's behavior or health easier, as you will have a baseline to compare against.

CONCLUSION

Congratulations, you've completed Kitten Boot Camp! Train your kitten like a boss, and you'll have a happy, healthy, and well-behaved kitten on your hands that would make Jack Byrnes proud! From basic commands to leash training, we've covered it all. And if you're dealing with destructive behavior, remember that positive reinforcement is the key to success. So put away those spray bottles and yelling voices, and embrace the power of treats and toys.

But wait, there's more! Next, we'll discuss the importance of spaying and neutering your kitten. Trust me, it's a topic you will want to take advantage of. So, get ready to learn all about the benefits of these procedures for your kitty's health and the community. See you on the other side!

1. Ollila, E. (2023, April 3). *Do's and Don'ts for Disciplining a Cat.* Hill's Pet Nutrition. https://www.hillspet.com/cat-care/routine-care/how-to-discipline-a-cat?lightboxfired=true
2. Hill's Pet Nutrition, Inc. (2022, August 30). *Steps for command training your kitten.* Hill's Pet Nutrition. https://www.hillspet.com/cat-care/training/kitten-command-training
3. Hodgson, S. (2022, May 19). 7 essential cat training tricks your kitty can really learn. *Daily Paws.* https://www.dailypaws.com/cats-kittens/cat-training/cat-training
4. O'Brien, C. (2022, August 30). *All About Your Cat's Sleeping Habits.* Hill's Pet Nutrition. https://www.hillspet.com/cat-care/behavior-appearance/are-cats-nocturnal

6

GETTING FIXED: SPAYING AND NEUTERING YOUR KITTEN

> This is Bob Barker reminding you to help control the pet population — have your pets spayed or neutered
>
> — BOB BARKER

S tray cats are a significant concern in the United States. Determining the exact number of stray cats is difficult, but various statistics and estimations can provide a general idea. According to these sources, it is estimated that the number of stray cats in the US could reach up to 70 million.[1]

These cats face numerous challenges, including hunger, disease, and overpopulation.

Also, their negative impact on the environment and wildlife must be addressed. According to an article on JSTOR Daily, domestic and feral cats significantly affect the environment. One study cited in the article found that domestic cats in the United States kill between 1.4 billion and 3.7 billion birds and between 6.9 billion and 20.7 billion mammals annually, with the majority of this damage being caused by unowned or feral cats.[2]

Cats can be wonderful pets, but they have a natural hunting instinct. When left to roam freely, they can devastate local ecosystems and wildlife by killing birds and mammals. Additionally, cats can spread diseases to other animals and humans, further compounding their negative environmental impact. To address this issue, spaying and neutering cats can reduce their numbers and improve their health and welfare.

So, you might be thinking, "My kitten will never become a stray cat because it's going to be an indoor cat." But here's the thing: according to a study conducted by the American Society for the Prevention of Cruelty to Animals, up to 15% of cat owners reported losing their cats over a five-year period. And to make matters worse, only 74% of those lost cats were eventually found.[3] That's why taking preventative measures is essential should your cat become lost.

In addition to the issue of overpopulation, spaying, and neutering also provide several health benefits for cats. Spaying and neutering can help ensure a longer and healthier life for our beloved kittens by reducing the risk of certain cancers and diseases.

In this chapter, we'll provide all the information you need about spaying and neutering your kitten. From the benefits to the age requirements to finding a qualified veterinarian, preparing for surgery, and post-surgery care - we've got you covered. So sit back, relax, and let's get started on this vital aspect of being a responsible cat owner.

LADIES FIRST: EXPLAINING SPAYING

Alright, let's talk about spaying your female kitten. Spaying is a surgical procedure that involves removing the ovaries and uterus of a female cat to prevent them from reproducing. Before the surgery, your kitten will typically undergo a physical examination to ensure they are healthy enough to undergo anesthesia. Your veterinarian may also recommend pre-operative blood work to check for underlying health conditions.

On the day of the surgery, your kitten will be given anesthesia to ensure that they are unconscious and feel no pain during the procedure. Once your kitten is asleep, the veterinarian will make a small incision in their abdomen and remove the ovaries and uterus. The incision is then closed with sutures or surgical glue.

After the surgery, your kitten will need time to recover from the anesthesia and the surgery itself. Your veterinarian will provide detailed instructions on how to care for your kitten during this time, including instructions on feeding, pain management, and monitoring for any signs of complications. It's important to note that this is a major surgery that should only be performed by a qualified veterinarian.

TIMING IS EVERYTHING: AGE REQUIREMENTS FOR SPAYING

You might be asking yourself, "When should I spay my kitten?" Spaying kittens as young as eight weeks old is generally considered safe. It is recommended to schedule the surgery before the cat reaches five months of age to eliminate the possibility of pregnancy.[4] However, the ideal age for spaying your kitten may vary depending on their breed, health status, and other factors. Therefore, it's best to consult your veterinarian to determine the best age for spaying your kitten.

BENEFITS OF SPAYING YOUR KITTEN

First and foremost, spaying can reduce the risk of your kitten developing reproductive diseases such as pyometra. These severe conditions can lead to life-threatening complications, so taking steps to prevent them is crucial. Also, spaying your kitten can reduce the risk of certain types of cancer. For example, spaying before the first heat cycle can significantly reduce the risk of mammary cancer. In fact, cats spayed before 6 months have a 7-times reduction in risk compared to intact cats.[5]

Another benefit of spaying is that it can prevent unwanted litters. This is especially important if you have multiple cats or stray cats in your neighborhood. The last thing you want is to contribute to the homeless cat population, which, as already mentioned, is a significant issue in many communities.

THE BIG SNIP: EXPLAINING NEUTERING

Neutering, also known as castration, is a surgical procedure that involves removing the testicles of a male cat to prevent them from reproducing. Just like with spaying, this is a major surgery that should only be performed by a qualified veterinarian.

Before the surgery, your veterinarian will typically perform a physical exam and may recommend pre-operative blood work to check for any underlying health conditions. They may also recommend fasting your kitten for a certain period before the surgery.

On the day of the surgery, your kitten will be given anesthesia to ensure that they are unconscious and feel no pain during the procedure. Once your kitten is asleep, the veterinarian will make a small incision in the scrotum and remove the testicles. The incision is then closed with sutures or surgical glue.

After the surgery, your kitten will need time to recover from the anesthesia and the surgery itself. Your veterinarian will provide detailed instructions on how to care for your kitten during this time, including instructions on feeding, pain management, and monitoring for any signs of complications.

It's essential to keep your kitten calm and restrict their activity during recovery to ensure that their incision site heals properly. In addition, your veterinarian typically schedules a follow-up appointment to check your kitten's progress and remove sutures.

TIMING IS EVERYTHING: AGE REQUIREMENTS FOR NEUTERING

So, when should you neuter your kitten? Just like with spaying, neutering kittens as young as eight weeks old is generally considered safe. It is recommended to schedule the surgery before the cat reaches five months of age to potentially prevent urine spraying.[6] However, just like with spaying, the ideal age for neutering may vary depending on your kitten's breed, health status, and other factors. Consult with your veterinarian to determine the best age for neutering your kitten.

THE BENEFITS OF THE BIG SNIP: WHY NEUTERING YOUR KITTEN IS A MUST

Now, let's talk about the benefits of neutering your kitten. First and foremost, neutering can prevent unwanted litters. This is especially important if you have multiple cats or stray cats in your neighborhood. It's important to remember that male cats can impregnate numerous females in a short amount of time, so neutering can greatly help control the stray cat population.

Another benefit of neutering your kitten is that it can reduce the risk of certain types of cancer. For example, neutering can reduce the risk of testicular cancer and can also reduce the risk of prostate cancer.[7] Additionally, neutering can reduce the risk of certain behavioral issues, such as spraying and roaming, which are often related to the male cat's mating behavior.

Finally, neutering can also reduce aggressive behavior in male cats. This is because neutering minimizes the production of certain hormones that can cause male cats to be more territorial and aggressive.

A CUT ABOVE THE REST: FINDING THE RIGHT VETERINARIAN

We briefly discussed this in Chapter 3, but it's worth repeating for the sake of this conversation. Imagine for a moment that you are the one getting this surgery. You wouldn't want just anyone performing the procedure, would you? Instead, you'd want a qualified doctor with experience and expertise in the field to care for you.

Well, the same goes for your feline friend. Your cat deserves the same level of care and attention that you would want for yourself. So, it's crucial to find a qualified veterinarian with experience performing these surgeries to ensure your cat's safety and comfort during and after the procedure. So let's make sure to give our cats the same level of care and attention that we would demand for ourselves...unless, of course, you're into DIY surgery, but I don't think that's recommended for anyone, cat or human! But, trust me, your cat will thank you for it (even if they don't show it in the most obvious way).

QUESTIONS TO ASK YOUR VETERINARIAN

When finding a veterinarian to perform your kitten's spay or neuter surgery, asking the right questions is vital in choosing a qualified and experienced professional. Here are some questions you can ask:

- How many spay or neuter surgeries have you performed on kittens?
- What is your success rate with these procedures?
- Are you licensed and certified to perform spay and neuter surgeries?
- What type of anesthesia do you use, and how do you ensure the safety of my kitten during the procedure?
- How long will the procedure take, and what is the expected recovery time?
- What type of pain management will be provided for my kitten during and after the surgery?
- What should I expect in terms of post-operative care and follow-up appointments?
- What are the potential risks or complications of the surgery, and how are these addressed?
- Do you offer additional services or resources for spay/neuter surgery, such as discounted programs or educational materials?

By asking these questions and ensuring that you feel comfortable with the veterinarian's responses, you can feel confident in choosing the right professional to perform your kitten's spay or neuter surgery.

THE COST OF RESPONSIBLE PET OWNERSHIP

When it comes to spaying or neutering your cat, you might wonder how much it will cost. Well, the answer is that it can vary quite a bit depending on where you live, which veterinary clinic you choose, and the age and health of your kitty.

The cost of spaying a cat may vary but typically ranges from $300 to $500 for a female cat and around $200 for neutering a male cat when performed at a private, full-service veterinary practice.[8] But don't let the price tag scare you off - spaying and neutering your cat is a vital part of responsible pet ownership, and there are ways to make it more affordable.

SAVING YOUR WALLET AND THE FELINE POPULATION

Several resources are available to help pet owners find discounted spay/neuter services. One option is to search for veterinary clinics that offer low-cost spay/neuter programs. You can also check with animal welfare organizations or non-profit groups in your area, such as the Humane Society or the ASPCA, as they often offer affordable spay/neuter services or vouchers to help offset the cost. Here are some resources to help you get started:

- ASPCA Spay/Neuter Programs: https://www.aspca. org/pet-care/spayneuter
- Humane Society Spay/Neuter Services: https:// www.humanesociety.org/resources/are-you- having-trouble-affording-your-pet

Ultimately, the cost of spaying or neutering your cat is a

small price to pay when you consider the long-term benefits for your kitty's health and the well-being of your community. So don't let the cost deter you - talk to your vet or local animal welfare group to find an affordable option that works for you and your kitten.

THE CALM BEFORE THE SNIP: PRE-SURGERY INSTRUCTIONS

Your veterinarian will provide instructions on what to do before the surgery, including when to stop feeding your kitten and when to arrive at the clinic. These instructions may vary depending on the age and health of your kitten, so it's essential to follow them carefully.

PREPARING YOUR KITTEN FOR THE SURGERY

You can help your kitten prepare for the surgery by ensuring they are clean, comfortable, and relaxed. Make sure their fur is free of tangles and mats. Keep them in a warm and comfortable environment leading up to the surgery, and try to keep their stress levels low.

Typically, cats should not eat or drink anything for at least 8-12 hours before the procedure. This helps prevent vomiting or other complications during the surgery.

PREPARING YOUR HOME FOR POST-SURGERY RECOVERY

Before bringing your kitten home after the surgery, you'll want to ensure their recovery area is set up and ready to go. This may include a comfortable bed, a litter box, food and water, and any medications or supplies your veterinarian has prescribed.

PILLOW FORTS AND PTERODACTYL SOUNDS: WHAT TO EXPECT AFTER SURGERY

It's important to remember that every cat is unique; some may react differently to anesthesia than others. In fact, when my own cat Mouse was spayed, she had a bit of a rough time post-surgery. She was aggressive and mean, making these weird noises that sounded like she was channeling her inner pterodactyl. To make matters worse, she couldn't stand or walk for a long time and wobbled around, trying to swat at my wife and me. It was quite a sight to see!

Fortunately, we were prepared for this possibility and had set up a cozy pillow fort for Mouse to rest and recover in. We let her take it easy and monitored her closely. The next morning, to our relief, she was almost entirely back to her normal self.

So don't be alarmed if your cat reacts differently to anesthesia than expected. Just be prepared, watch them closely, and ensure they have a comfortable and quiet place to rest and recover. And who knows, maybe your cat will have a funny story to share too!

As for your specific cat's spay or neuter surgery, it is crucial to provide proper post-operative care to ensure a smooth and comfortable recovery. Your veterinarian will give detailed instructions on caring for your kitten after surgery, but here are some general guidelines to remember.

- Limiting their physical activity for a few days to a week
- Monitoring their behavior and appetite
- Giving any prescribed medications
- Keeping the surgical site clean and dry

You should also schedule a follow-up appointment with your vet for a check-up and contact them if you notice any concerning changes or symptoms.

THE WATCHFUL EYE: POTENTIAL COMPLICATIONS AND WHAT TO LOOK OUT FOR

While spaying and neutering procedures are standard and usually safe, there is always a risk of complications. It's essential to be aware of these potential complications and to contact your veterinarian immediately if you notice any of the following symptoms:

- **Persistent lethargy or loss of appetite:** Your kitten may appear tired and uninterested in food. This could be a sign of an infection or other complication, so it is essential to contact your veterinarian immediately.
- **Swelling, discharge, or redness around the surgical site**: These symptoms may indicate an infection or an allergic reaction to the surgical materials used. If you notice any of these symptoms, contact your veterinarian immediately.

- **Excessive bleeding or discharge from the surgical site**: A small amount of discharge or bleeding is normal after surgery, but if you notice excessive amounts, it could be a sign of a complication. Contact your veterinarian right away if you notice this symptom.
- **Signs of pain or discomfort**: Your kitten may exhibit signs of pain or discomfort, such as whining, limping, or reluctance to move. This could be a sign of a complication or infection and should be addressed by your veterinarian as soon as possible.

In general, it's important to closely monitor your kitten after the surgery and follow your veterinarian's instructions for aftercare. Being vigilant and attentive to your kitten's symptoms can help ensure a smooth recovery after their spay or neuter procedure.

CONCLUSION

While spaying and neutering may seem daunting, with a bit of preparation and care, your kitten can fully recover and return to their mischievous antics in no time.

Remember, as responsible pet owners, it's our duty to ensure our kittens stay healthy and happy. Spaying and neutering your kitten benefits their health and helps control the stray cat population. So let's continue to do our part and give our cats the care they deserve.

In the next chapter, we'll explore all the exciting adventures you can have with your kitten indoors and outdoors. We'll cover everything you need to know, from hiking to playdates to keep your kitten entertained and engaged. So get ready to have some fun and create memories with your furry friend!

1. Advanced Care Veterinary Hospital. (2022b, May 10). *How Many Stray Cats are in the United States?* https://advancedpetvet.com/2022/05/09/how-many-stray-cats-are-in-the-united-states/
2. Wills, M. (2017). The environmental danger of outdoor cats. *JSTOR Daily.* https://daily.jstor.org/environmental-danger-outdoor-cats/
3. American Society for the Prevention of Cruelty to Animals. (n.d.). *How Many Pets are Lost? How Many Find Their Way Home? ASPCA Survey Has Answers.* ASPCA. https://www.aspca.org/about-us/press-releases/how-many-pets-are-lost-how-many-find-their-way-home-aspca-survey-has-answers
4. American Veterinary Medical Association. (n.d.). *Spaying and neutering.* https://www.avma.org/resources-tools/pet-owners/petcare/spaying-and-neutering
5. American College of Veterinary Surgeons. (2023, June 29). *Mammary Tumors - American College of Veterinary Surgeons.* https://www.acvs.org/small-animal/mammary-tumors
6. American Veterinary Medical Association. (n.d.). *Spaying and neutering.* https://www.avma.org/resources-tools/pet-owners/petcare/spaying-and-neutering
7. American Veterinary Medical Association. (n.d.-b). *Spaying and neutering.* https://www.avma.org/resources/pet-owners/petcare/spaying-and-neutering

8. PetMD Editorial. (2016, March 10). *How Much Does it Cost to Spay a Cat?* PetMD. https://www.petmd.com/cat/care/evr_ct_how-much-does-it-cost-to-spay-a-cat

7

KITTEN QUESTS: EMBARKING ON ADVENTURES WITH YOUR NEW COMPANION

> Time spent with a cat is never wasted
>
> — JEAN COCTEAU

Y ou've prepared your home, trained your kitten, and now it's time for some serious adventuring. But where to start? Fear not, my fellow feline fanatic, for this chapter is here to guide you through the exciting world of outdoor and indoor adventures with your kitten.

Kittens are born explorers; whether climbing a tree or jumping on the couch, they love discovering new things. But before letting your little adventurer loose in the great outdoors, ensure you've taken all the necessary safety precautions. And don't worry; we'll walk you through it all.

From outdoor hikes to indoor playtime, this chapter has got you covered. We'll give you tips and tricks for keeping your kitten entertained and engaged while ensuring they stay safe and healthy. So grab your leash, pack some treats, and prepare for some unforgettable adventures with your furry best friend. Meow!

CONQUERING THE WILD OUTDOORS WITH YOUR KITTEN

Ah, the great outdoors! A place for adventure, excitement, and fresh air. And why should your furry feline friend miss out on all the fun? Taking your kitten on outdoor expeditions can be a thrilling experience for both of you, but keeping safety in mind is essential.

First and foremost, ensure that your kitten is comfortable being outside. Some cats are simply not cut out for outdoor adventures and may prefer the comfort and security of their indoor surroundings. If your kitten seems anxious or skittish, it's best to stick to indoor playtime for now. If your kitten is ready for some outdoor exploration, make sure to take the necessary precautions.

SAFETY TIPS FOR OUTDOOR ADVENTURES

The first step is to identify potential hazards in your environment. Busy streets, bodies of water, and other dangerous animals are some of the most common risks you may encounter when exploring the great outdoors with your kitten. Make sure you choose a safe location for your adventure, and keep your kitten on a body harness and leash or in a secure carrier to prevent them from wandering off into dangerous territory.

It's also important to be prepared for any emergencies that may arise. Carrying a first aid kit and knowing your vet's contact information can be a lifesaver in case of accidents or injuries. Additionally, ensure your kitten is up-to-date on vaccinations and microchipped so that you can quickly locate them if they get lost. Now let's talk about some exciting outdoor activities you can enjoy with your kitten!

HIKING AND BACKPACKING

Hiking and backpacking can be great ways to explore nature with your cat. However, taking necessary precautions and bringing the right gear for your furry friend is essential.

Firstly, ensure your cat is comfortable walking on a leash

and wearing a harness before embarking on a hiking trip. A well-fitted harness and leash are essential to ensure your cat's safety while on the trail. Consider also carrying a pet carrier or backpack to provide your cat with a comfortable place to rest during breaks or if they become tired.

When it comes to gear, make sure to bring plenty of food and water for both you and your cat. Plan to carry 1.5 to 2.5 pounds of dry food (or 2,500 to 4,500 calories) per person per day.[1] Your cat will need food, water, and a collapsible bowl to eat and drink from. In addition, it's vital to bring enough water to stay hydrated, especially in warmer weather, and to refill your bottles as necessary.

Checking the weather forecast before heading out is crucial for your safety and your cat's. If extreme weather conditions are predicted, postponing your hike and choosing another day is best. You can check for park alerts and trail closures on the park's website.[2]

In addition to the bare essentials, it's a good idea to bring navigation tools such as a map and compass, a first-aid kit, a knife or multi-tool, and insect-repellent clothing to protect against mosquitoes and other bugs.[3]

Remember, your cat's safety and comfort should be your top priority when hiking or backpacking together. Take breaks as needed, and be prepared to turn back if your cat becomes tired or shows signs of discomfort. Then, you and your feline friend can enjoy the great outdoors together with the right gear and precautions.

CAMPING

Camping with your kitten can be a fun and memorable outdoor adventure. However, before you head out, choosing a camping location that allows pets and following all camping regulations is crucial. In addition, when camping with your kitten, you want to ensure they stay cozy and warm. Bringing a warm blanket or bed and a sleeping pad can help your kitten stay comfortable throughout the night. You can also get a small tent for your kitten to sleep in if they prefer a more enclosed space.

When packing for your camping trip with your kitten, it's important to pack layers of breathable, water-resistant clothing. This will not only keep you comfortable, but it will also help keep your kitten warm and dry. Wool, fleece, and synthetic materials are great options, but avoid cotton clothing as it does not retain warmth when wet.

In addition to packing warm clothing, it's essential to bring plenty of food and water for both you and your kitten. Bring extra food and water in case of emergency or unexpected circumstances. Also, consider getting a collapsible bowl for your kitten to drink out of.

While camping with your kitten, remember to bring some fun toys and games to play with. Remember to also get a sturdy leash and harness for your kitten to safely explore their surroundings.

Overall, camping with your kitten can be a great way to bond and create lasting memories. Just take the necessary precautions and follow all camping regulations to ensure a safe and enjoyable trip.

BREWED FOR TWO: THE BENEFITS OF BREWERY OUTINGS WITH YOUR KITTEN

Perhaps this is just me, but maybe you can relate. I love to frequent my local breweries. Picture this: You're sitting on a sunny patio, sipping on a crisp beer, and your furry feline friend is lounging at your feet, basking in the sun. Sounds like the perfect afternoon, doesn't it? That's why taking your kitten to breweries that allow pets is a great idea.

First and foremost, bringing your kitten to breweries is an excellent opportunity for social-ization. Kittens that are exposed to new environments, sounds, and people at an early age are more likely to become well-adjusted and friendly adult cats. So why not introduce your kitten to the exciting world of breweries? They'll learn to adapt to new situations and people, and you'll have a social butterfly of a cat on your hands.

But it's not just your kitten who benefits from these outings. Breweries often share photos of cats on their premises, and who doesn't want their furry friend to become Instagram famous? Cats are rarer in brewery photos than dogs, so your kitten will stand out from the crowd. You'll have plenty of photo ops for your social media pages.

> **Pro Tip:** If you plan to start a social media page for your cat, bring a printed QR code for others to easily find your cat's page, garner new followers, and get your kitten's pres-ence out faster.

You might even inspire other cat owners to take their kittens on brewery adventures too.

And let's not forget about the fun factor. The ultimate

relaxation combination is drinking a cold beer while snuggling with your kitten. You get to indulge in your favorite beverage while enjoying the company of your furry friend. What could be better than that?

So, taking your kitten to breweries that allow pets is a win-win situation. Your kitten benefits from socialization and exposure to new environments, and the brewery gets unique content to showcase your cute cat on their social media, and you both get to enjoy some much-needed relaxation time. So why not plan your next brewery adventure with your furry friend? Cheers to good beer and good company!

INDOOR EXPLORATION AND PLAYTIME

Who says indoor life has to be boring? If you want to keep your furry feline friend entertained, there are plenty of options for indoor activities that are just as fun as outdoor adventures. Not to mention, you'll have peace of mind knowing your kitten is safe and sound within the comfort of your own home.

TOYS

Kittens are playful and curious animals, and it's essential to provide them with a variety of toys and activities to keep them entertained and stimulated. By introducing new games and toys, you can encourage your kitten's natural behaviors, such as chasing, pouncing, and hunting, which can also help them develop their physical and mental abilities.

DIY toys are an excellent option to keep your kitten engaged without breaking the bank. You can create fun and safe toys using household items such as cardboard boxes, paper bags, and old socks. Cardboard boxes can be turned into tunnels, hideouts, or scratching posts, while paper bags can be filled with crumpled paper or toys for your kitten to explore. Old socks can be stuffed with catnip or other toys to create a soft and playful toy for your kitten to toss around.

Interactive toys are also a great way to mentally stimulate your kitten. Toys like puzzle feeders or treat dispensers can challenge your kitten's mind and encourage them to use their natural problem-solving abilities. These toys also promote a healthy eating pace and can help reduce behavior problems that stem from boredom or overeating.

PLAYDATES

Hosting playdates for your kitten can be a fun and exciting experience for both you and your kitten. Not only does it provide them with physical exercise, but it also helps with socialization, which is essential for their development.

When introducing your kitten to other cats, it's crucial to do so gradually and in a controlled environment. Keep in mind that cats are territorial animals, and introducing a new cat too quickly or aggressively can lead to conflicts and stress for both cats. So instead, start by allowing them to sniff and investigate each other through a closed door or barrier for a few days before letting them interact face-to-face.

It's also important to supervise the playdate and keep an eye out for any signs of aggression or tension between the cats. Signs of aggression can include hissing, growling, and swatting. If you notice any of these behaviors, it's best to separate the cats and try again later.

Aside from introducing your kitten to other cats, you can

also try introducing them to other friendly pets in the household, such as dogs or rabbits. This can provide them with new experiences and opportunities to learn how to interact with different animals.

Hosting playdates and introducing your kitten to other pets should always be done in a safe and controlled environment to ensure a positive experience for everyone involved.

BUILDING AN OBSTACLE COURSE

Cats are natural explorers, and their inquisitive nature can lead them to get into mischief around the house. Building an indoor obstacle course for your cat can provide them with a stimulating environment to explore, play, and expend energy.

The first step in creating an indoor obstacle course is identifying the space you want to use. A room with ample space and minimal clutter is ideal, such as a spare bedroom, home office, or basement. Once you have selected the area, you can begin to plan the layout and design of the course.

When designing the course, consider incorporating elements that stimulate your cat's senses, such as tunnels, scratching posts, and perches. Tunnels can be made from PVC pipes, cardboard boxes, or large fabric tubes. Scratching posts can be made using carpet, rope, or wood, and perches can be created by attaching shelves or platforms to the walls.

To encourage your cat to use the obstacle course, consider adding treats and toys throughout the course. This will encourage your cat to explore and navigate the course, making it a fun and rewarding experience.

HIGH AND MIGHTY: THE PSYCHOLOGY BEHIND A CAT'S OBSESSION WITH PERCHING

Building an obstacle course could also have the added benefit of giving your kitten a high location to retreat to. Cats have an innate desire to climb and perch in high places. This behavior is a product of their instincts as both predators and prey.

Being in high spots gives cats a better view of their surroundings and increases their chances of detecting prey or predators. Additionally, high perches provide cats a sense of security and a private space to retreat when overwhelmed. Sometimes they just need a little personal space to unwind and relax, and what better place to do that than up high, where they can survey their kingdom from a safe distance?

It's not uncommon for cats to climb to high places in our homes, such as bookshelves, window sills, or even the top of the refrigerator. Providing them with designated climbing and perching areas can satisfy their natural instincts and keep them off potentially dangerous areas such as countertops or tables. Consider incorporating cat trees, shelves, or window perches into your home to encourage your feline friend to ascend to higher locations.

In my household, we gave Mouse a two-foot staircase that led from the kitchen table to the top of the kitchen cabinets, which she loved to retreat to whenever we had friends over. Of course, she eventually came down to be with the group, but having that place she called her own to sit and watch meant a lot to her and made her feel safe and in control.

Safety is paramount when building an obstacle course or high place for your kitten. Ensure that all elements are securely anchored and that there are no sharp edges or potential hazards that could cause injury to your pet. Also, be sure to supervise your cat while using the course and remove any objects or materials that may threaten their safety.

CONCLUSION

One thing to keep in mind is that kittens tend to be creatures of routine and prefer the comfort of their familiar surroundings. They feel safe and secure when they have a set schedule and know what to expect from their day. However, if you desire to venture out of the home to explore the world with them, whether it be a trip to the park or a car ride, they will bond with you and look to you as their comfort and constant in unfamiliar situations. You become their safe haven and the source of reassurance when they feel anxious or unsure.

However, it's important to remember that every kitten is different; some may not enjoy going out and adventuring as much as others. Therefore, if your kitten seems stressed or uncomfortable in new situations, it's best to respect their preferences and provide them with a safe and comfortable environment at home.

Congratulations! You're now ready to explore the great outdoors and have some indoor adventures with your kitten. Whether you choose to hike, camp, play in the park, or hit up the local brew pub, make sure to have fun and enjoy the company.

However, as much as we love our kittens, we must also make some tough ethical decisions. In the next chapter, we will delve into the controversial topic of declawing cats. We will examine the arguments for and against the procedure and explore the potential health effects and anatomy of declawing. It's a somber topic but an important one that kitten owners must consider carefully. Let's dive in.

1. Gilbert, G. (n.d.). *How to plan a backpacking trip*. REI. https://www.rei.com/learn/expert-advice/backpack-planning.html
2. National Park Service. (2020, August 7). *Hike Smart (U.S. National Park Service)*. https://www.nps.gov/articles/hiking-safety.htm
3. Kehoe, J. (n.d.). *Day hiking Essentials checklist*. REI. https://www.rei.com/learn/expert-advice/day-hiking-checklist.html

8

THE CLAW CONTROVERSY: UNDERSTANDING THE ETHICAL DEBATE ON DECLAWING

> Declawing is something that is done simply for human convenience—to essentially mutilate a living being to protect a couch. That is just crazy to me. Some compromise is needed for living with an animal
>
> — JACKSON GALAXY

Declawing is a surgical procedure involving amputating a cat's toes at the last bone (distal phalanx), which removes the attached claws. It is often done to prevent scratching of furniture or injury to humans.[1] However, the ethical debate surrounding declawing raises questions about whether it is a humane or cruel practice.

Supporters of declawing argue that it is a necessary measure to protect furniture and prevent injury to humans. In addition, they believe it is a humane solution to prevent cats from being surrendered to shelters or being euthanized due to destructive behavior.[2]

On the other hand, opponents of declawing argue that the procedure can cause physical and emotional distress to the cat and should be considered a form of animal cruelty. They argue that cats rely on their claws for self-defense, balance, and normal behavior and that declawing interferes with these natural instincts. Additionally, declawing can lead to chronic pain, arthritis, and behavioral issues.[3]

To better understand the debate, it is essential to take a closer look at the procedure itself and its effects on a cat's anatomy.

ANATOMY OF DECLAWING

Cats are classified as digitigrade animals because they walk on their toes with the rest of their foot lifted off the ground. This means that their metatarsals, or the bones that connect their toes to their ankles, touch the ground while the rest of their foot, including the heel, remains elevated. The digitigrade stance allows cats to move quickly and quietly and to maintain balance and agility while hunting prey or climbing.

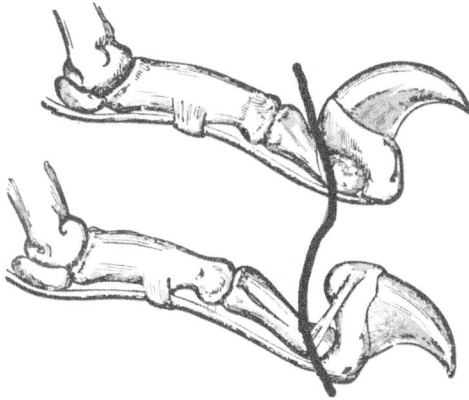

FIG. 7.—UPPER FIGURE : CLAW AT REST, HELD BACK
BY ELASTIC LIGAMENT.   LOWER FIGURE : CLAW DRAWN
DOWN BY CONTRACTION OF TENDON BELOW, ELASTIC
LIGAMENT STRETCHED, AND CLAW PROTRUDING.

Declawing, also known as onychectomy, is an elective
surgical procedure that involves amputating the last joint of
each toe, including the claw and the surrounding bone, which
removes the cat's toe bones, tendons, and nerves.[4] The surgery
uses a scalpel, laser, or guillotine clipper, and each method
carries its own risks and potential complications. This procedure is comparable to removing the first finger bone in
humans. However, the analogy is not perfect and breaks down
because humans do not walk on their fingertips. Because of the
digitigrade nature of cats, declawing significantly affects a
cat's ability to walk, jump, and defend itself. [5]

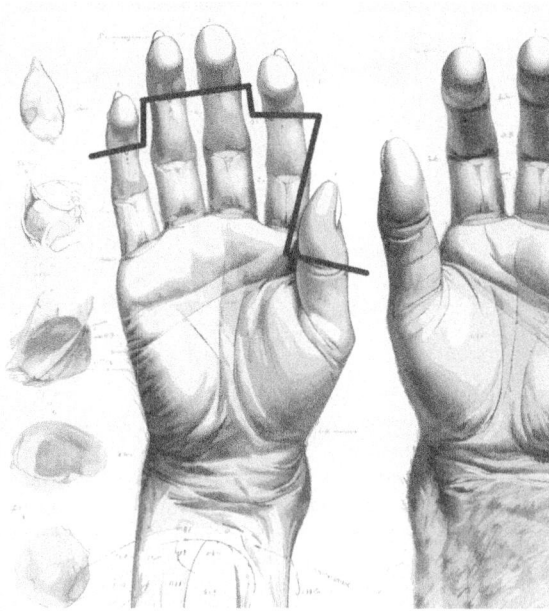

Cats are also deprived of many other natural behaviors, including marking their territory appropriately, stretching their back muscles, climbing trees to escape predators, kneading during affectionate moments, and engaging in play and hunting activities. By declawing cats, their natural instincts and behaviors are compromised, which can negatively impact their physical and mental health.[6]

Moreover, just like human amputees, declawed cats can experience phantom limb pain when their nervous system sends pain signals to the brain from the missing digits, even when they are no longer there.[7] The phantom limb pain can persist for a long time, and it's one of the many adverse effects of declawing that opponents point to when arguing against the practice.

The recovery process is a critical component of a successful outcome. After the procedure, the cat should be kept in a quiet, stress-free environment for proper healing. Pain medication and antibiotics may also be prescribed to manage pain and prevent infection.[8] It's worth noting that declawed cats may require a different type of litter to avoid discomfort.[9]

In addition, it's essential to understand that declawing can have long-term effects on a cat's health and behavior. For example, one study found that 42% of declawed cats had ongoing long-term pain, and about a quarter of the cats had behavior changes such as increased biting and litter box avoidance.[10]

THE AFTERMATH OF DECLAWING: UNDERSTANDING THE PHYSICAL AND EMOTIONAL EFFECTS ON CATS

In addition to chronic pain and mobility issues, declawed cats are also at a significant disadvantage in defending themselves. Without their claws, they cannot climb or scratch, which are natural instinctive behaviors that cats use to protect themselves from predators or escape danger. The inability to climb can leave declawed cats vulnerable to other predators if they accidentally get outside. This is especially concerning for indoor-only cats unfamiliar with the dangers of the outdoors.[11]

Furthermore, removing the claws can also impact a cat's behavior and personality. Cats may become anxious, aggressive, or withdrawn due to the physical and emotional trauma caused by the declawing procedure. This can lead to a breakdown in the bond between the cat and its owner, causing further stress and discomfort for the kitten.

It's also worth noting that declawing is illegal or restricted in many countries, including the United Kingdom, Australia, and several European countries. Some U.S. cities and states have also banned or restricted the practice. In addition, in recent years, more and more veterinarians and animal welfare organizations have spoken out against declawing, citing the adverse health effects and ethical concerns. As an alternative, they recommend behavior modification techniques or providing cats with appropriate scratching surfaces to redirect their natural scratching behavior.

Overall, while declawing may seem like a convenient solution for cat owners, it can have severe and long-lasting adverse effects on the cat's physical health, behavior, and ability to defend itself. Therefore, cat owners must consider the potential consequences before opting for this procedure and explore alternative options for managing their cat's scratching behavior.

ALTERNATIVES TO DECLAWING

Declawing is a permanent and irreversible procedure that can cause physical and emotional harm to cats. Fortunately, many alternatives to declawing can effectively prevent furniture damage and protect humans from cat scratches. Regular nail trimming is one of the most effective methods for keeping a cat's claws short and preventing damage to furniture. Trimming a cat's claws every few weeks removes the sharp tips, and the cat is less likely to scratch furniture or other surfaces. However, learning how to properly trim a cat's nails is essential to avoid accidentally injuring them. We already discussed this in Chapter 3, but it wouldn't hurt to revisit the topic in light of this discussion:

- Make sure to use proper cat nail clippers and avoid using human nail clippers or scissors, which can cause damage to the cat's nails.
- Gently hold the cat's paw and locate the pink part of the nail, which is the "quick," and avoid cutting into it. If you're unsure where the quick is located, it's best to trim small amounts at a time.
- Reward your cat with treats or affection after each successful nail-trimming session to create a positive association with the experience

Providing scratching posts and teaching cats to use them is another effective alternative to declawing. Cats naturally scratch to mark their territory, stretch their muscles, and keep their claws in good condition. Cats can satisfy their natural urge to scratch without damaging furniture or other surfaces by providing a variety of scratching posts in different materials and textures. It's vital to place scratching posts in visible and accessible areas where cats spend most of their time.

Another alternative to declawing is the use of Soft Paws. Soft Paws are a type of plastic nail cap that is glued onto the cat's claws. They are easy to apply and can last for several weeks. However, while Soft Paws can prevent damage to furniture and other objects, they should be seen as a last resort rather than a first line of defense against scratching. It is important to remember that scratching is a natural behavior for cats and plays a vital role in their physical and emotional well-being. Providing cats with appropriate scratching surfaces and redirecting their behavior towards those surfaces can often resolve unwanted scratching behavior without needing nail caps.

MOUSE'S CHAIR

I would like to share a quick story to foot-stomp this point: as Megan and I were unpacking after moving to New York cross country from Arizona, we made a quick stop at the store to pick up some essentials. We were already tired and stressed from the move, so we didn't put too much thought into the folding chair with the fabric seat that we threw in our cart.

Fast forward a few weeks, and we're finally settled into our new home. Our cat Mouse had surprisingly adjusted to the new space, but we quickly noticed she needed a good scratching post. That's when she discovered the folding chair.

At first, we were a bit frustrated that she was scratching up the fabric on our brand-new chair. But then we realized she wasn't just scratching it up; she was claiming it as her own. So we watched as she stretched out her little paws and dug her claws into the fabric, her eyes closed in pure bliss.

Mouse found comfort and security in that folding chair over the course of many other moves, and it became her go-to spot for scratching when she was anxious or stressed. The best part is that I am able to witness the raw, fierce predator that is inside of her manifest in a way that is satisfying to her and makes her happy while still not destroying the furniture that I actually care about.

The truth is, even a modest $20 chair can hold immeasurable value for a kitten. It's simply not worth robbing them of something as vital as their claws to protect a mere piece of furniture.

CONCLUSION

If you live in a state or country that still allows for declawing kittens, you have a very important decision to make. While it might be tempting to declaw a kitten to prevent them from scratching, it's essential to understand that declawing is an amputation procedure that is extremely painful and can lead to long-term physical and behavioral problems for your kitten. While dealing with a kitten's scratching behavior can be challenging, the reward of a happy and healthy cat is well worth the effort. With patience and positive reinforcement, you can train your kitten to use their scratching surfaces and develop good habits that will benefit them for the rest of their lives.

---

1. Brown, J. (2022, November 30). *Declawing cats: What you need to know.* Cats.com. https://cats.com/declawing-cats

2. Animal Legal Defense Fund. (2023, August 2). *Declawing Cats - Animal Legal Defense Fund.* https://aldf.org/issue/declawing-cats/
3. American Veterinary Medical Association. (2019, July 23). *American Veterinary Medical Association.* https://www.avma.org/sites/default/files/resources/declawing_bgnd.pdf
4. Brown, J. (2022b, November 30). *Declawing cats: What you need to know.* Cats.com. https://cats.com/declawing-cats
5. Halperin, I. (n.d.). *How are cats declawed, and is it painful?* The Conversation. https://theconversation.com/how-are-cats-declawed-and-is-it-painful-119579
6. Galaxy, J. (2023, July 25). *Declawing: Don't do it!* Jackson Galaxy. https://www.jacksongalaxy.com/blogs/news/declawing-don-t-do-it?_pos=1&_sid=086d8caea&_ss=r
7. Halperin, I. (n.d.). *How are cats declawed, and is it painful?* The Conversation. https://theconversation.com/how-are-cats-declawed-and-is-it-painful-119579
8. Sakura, L. (2023, March 22). *Cat Declawing: Pros, Cons, and Safer Alternatives.* Reader's Digest. https://www.rd.com/article/cat-declawing/
9. Halperin, I. (n.d.). *How are cats declawed, and is it painful?* The Conversation. https://theconversation.com/how-are-cats-declawed-and-is-it-painful-119579
10. Halperin, I. (n.d.). *How are cats declawed, and is it painful?* The Conversation. https://theconversation.com/how-are-cats-declawed-and-is-it-painful-119579
11. Sakura, L. (2023, March 22). *Cat Declawing: Pros, Cons, and Safer Alternatives.* Reader's Digest. https://www.rd.com/article/cat-declawing/

AFTERWORD

> What greater gift than the love of a cat?
>
> — CHARLES DICKENS

Congratulations on becoming a kitten parent! You are about to embark on a journey filled with joy, love, and companionship. As you welcome your new feline friend into your home, observing and learning your kitten's personality and habits are essential. Spend time with your kitten and pay attention to their quirks and preferences. This will help you develop a deeper bond with them and make providing the best care possible easier. Kittens are wonderful pets that can bring much happiness into your life. However, it's important to remember that underneath their cute fuzzy exterior, they are, by nature, fierce predators and hunters. Kittens need to exercise those predator instincts and thus require plenty of playtime and mental stimulation to stay happy and healthy.

However, it's important to note that the information in this book is just the beginning. As your kitten grows and develops, their needs and preferences will change. Therefore, keeping up with your kitten's growth and adapting your care is vital.

It's essential to continue educating yourself about your kitten's needs throughout their life. Stay informed about new products, treatments, and care techniques to help you provide your kitten with the best possible life. Attend events at your local animal shelter or participate in online forums to connect with other cat parents and share information.

By staying informed and adapting to your kitten's changing needs, you can ensure they lead a healthy and fulfilling life. So, continue learning, growing, and enjoying this special bond between human and feline. Remember, you're not alone in this journey. Plenty of resources are available to help you become the best cat parent you can be. Experts from the ASPCA to your local animal shelter are ready and willing to answer your questions and offer guidance.

Finally, if you found this book helpful, please leave a review on Amazon by scanning the QR code. Not only will it help other new kitten parents find this book, but it will also make the author (ME) feel warm and fuzzy inside. After all, we're all in this together to give these furry creatures the best lives possible.

Leave a Review

So, welcome to the exciting and responsible world of kitten ownership. Enjoy this new adventure, and cherish the moments you share with your kitten! With love, patience, and a willingness to learn, you and your new feline friend will surely have a purrfectly happy life together.

Printed in Great Britain
by Amazon

51797410R00078